THE
SAN FRANCISCO
Thrift and Wisdom
ALMANAC

San Francisco's Native Wisdom!

Editor, **Walter Biller**

ISSN# 1053-1696   ISBN 0-9628427-1-0

THE SAN FRANCISCO ALMANAC

THE SAN FRANCISCO ALMANAC
1657 Waller Street #A
SF, CA 94117-2811

(415) 751-0657
In The City
1-800-352-5268

Copyright © 1992-1993
THE SAN FRANCISCO ALMANAC
Editor, Walter Biller

ISSN# 1053-1696
ISBN# 0-9628427-1-0

Distributed by L–S Distributors.
Call 1-800-654-7040 for wholesale,
1-800-352-5268 for retail orders.

"Native Wisdom!"

THE ALMANAC is a "stone soup" of sorts—people and businesses bring to it what they can offer, so that all may benefit. We devote our third annual issue's pages to SF's "Native Wisdom," bringing you the word on a myriad of great businesses and resources in San Francisco, everybody's favorite city.

To help us promote the activities of our community, paid sponsors contributed to this issue. They help keep the cover price low and improve our work so our readership can grow. We believe we attract a particularly fine group of people and businesses, and encourage readers to grab the ALMANAC next time they have donations or resources to offer, or if they are looking for a good business.

A publication lives and dies by three counts: the quality of its readers, its sponsors and its "product." We've worked hard to give our fine readers and sponsors, and our greater local community, the finest issue of THE SAN FRANCISCO ALMANAC to date. (On the first two counts, we feel we're in very good hands!) Please *do* tell your friends about us, and we encourage you to write or call anytime with ALMANAC reader suggestions.

Editor, **Walter Biller**

San Francisco's Native Wisdom!

THE SAN FRANCISCO ALMANAC

Thanks to the fine organizations, sponsors, writers and our many readers who contributed to this third ALMANAC issue...

For suggestions, comments, inquiries, advertising or retail distribution, contact the Editor at 751-0657 or 1-800-352-5268.

Now available at Waldenbooks, Brentano's, Tower Books & Magazines, and at better book & magazine stores throughout San Francisco and the Bay Area. Call for mail-order (free shipping) or for the store nearest you.

Editor and Manager
Walter Biller

Executive Editor
Maureen Caffrey

Production Consultant
Lillian Biller

Associate Editor
Michael Koenig

Graphics Editor/Illustrator
Elizabeth Newman

Special thanks to Lillian Biller for her important assistance. Thanks to Barbara Driscoll, Alice Besse, Guideline Publications and the SF Public Library for their extra consideration. To our readers—BRAVO!

This 3rd revised Edition of THE SAN FRANCISCO ALMANAC dedicated to the memory of Raymond H. Clary...

TABLE OF CONTENTS

Completely
New Index!
See Back Pages...

Over 1,500 activities!
SF's Native Wisdom!

and more . . .

Beach Blanket Babylon
Club Fugazi

All Things

SAN FRANCISCO

& Readers' Favorites from
The Almanac News

Share your "Native Wisdom"
with ALMANAC readers.
Write to:
THE SAN FRANCISCO ALMANAC,
1657 Waller Street #A, SF, CA
94117, or call 1-800-352-5268
and speak to Editor Walter
Biller. Thanks to all our fine
patrons for their assistance in
this third-year issue!

Bookmobile Angels

The Friends of the Public Library had raised about half of the $125,000 necessary to buy and outfit a new bookmobile when a lawyer called. A check was being prepared—for the balance still necessary to purchase the new bus/library for home-bound seniors. (The check's author would remain anonymous.) The bookmobile was real!

Bookstores and publishers are encouraged to call Friends at 557-4257 with offers of new books; call 557-4345 for bus schedule. Friends Director Jane Winslow thanks all those who gave money and valuable time to help make the new Bookmobile possible.

Academy Grill

The California Culinary Academy, a world-class cooking school, serves lunches weekdays from 11:30 a.m. - 1:45 p.m. at 625 Polk Street (at Turk). The lunch menu includes $7.95 blue-plate specials; fish, chicken and beef grill treats; sandwiches and clubs; 13

Build It and They Will Come...

Chuck Burkhardt, former pro boxing trainer from Newman's Gym (when it was located in the ballroom of the Cadillac Hotel) has a dream—to build a boxing program for Tenderloin kids.

"When Billy Newman was alive, we had a few boxing lessons for kids on Saturdays. If a Tenderloin business owner will donate some weekend space, we can get some of these kids off of the street and into the ring. Boxing builds better citizens," says Burkhardt.

Call Chuck at 621-4422 if you can help make this dream a reality for his kids. Let us know, too, if we can help.

wines, each priced at $13.00, and an incredibly tasty apple crisp. The energetic young staff offers white-linen service in a fun, upbeat setting. Italian and roast beef buffet dinners are also available. Call 771-1655. (Lunch available carry-out, too.)

Cathedral School For Boys NASA Project–Go!

Thanks to Ron King, whose son James is a Cathedral School for Boys student, the San Francisco school will be sending a space science experiment into deep orbit. The project, which is being developed by a number of the boys, explores how liquids behave under zero gravity. The results may help further NASA's mid-space refueling research.

Mr. King is an employee of Lockheed. He learned that another space project had been scrubbed and that a replacement was needed. Bonnie Germain of Cathedral School's thrift shop says all of the proud parents and kids will be watching the space shot in September.

Red's Java House

Red's is the popular little burger-shack under the Bay Bridge at Pier 30. Recently billboard ads have appeared: "You'll never find food like this at the best restaurants in Paris. Signed, Red." At publication, a burger and a "Bud" still cost $2.35, just the same as last year. Parking is a snap. Escape the roaring crowd, enjoy some afternoon sun and have a good burger at Red's. It's a different kind of downtown lunch-spot.

All-Year Christmas Cheer

Jack Early, a San Francisco advertising man, has sent millions of used Christmas and birthday cards to missionaires, churches and schools throughout the world. These organizations then remake them and use them for religious and artistic purposes. In some cases, they sell the remade cards for their charitable causes.

To recycle your cards this year, send them to Father Herbert A. Ward at St. Jude's Ranch for Children. All styles of cards are accepted.

Father Herbert A. Ward
St. Jude's Ranch for Children
PO Box 985
Boulder City, Nevada 89005

Mark parcel "Printed Matter–Used Greeting Cards—No Commercial Value—May Be Opened for Inspection."

Packages of greeting cards up to a maximum of 4 lbs. can be sent at the "Printed Matter" surface mail rate. For reference, 1 lb. is several dozen cards or more, and takes about $3 in stamps.

Well worth the postage in holiday cheer. Thanks, Jack, for the effort. Happy Holidays to you and yours!

Share the Wealth

Editor, Ginny Kolmar

Many San Franciscans will remember *Share the Wealth,* an energetic monthly newsletter series that featured special bargains, better restaurants, good shops and great local services. The publication thrived for almost twenty years, with contributing writers and readers from all over the Bay Area offering their favorite suggestions.

Publisher Ginny Kolmar commanded radio and TV time-slots, too, sharing her extensive editor's potpourri with avid listeners and viewers everywhere.

We were very lucky to have had the opportunity to speak with Ginny recently after a pleased reader brought her name up. (Ginny asked us to *please* emphasize to her and our beloved readers that *STW* closed its doors in 1989. *STW* fans might keep an eye on The ALMANAC for future contributions.)

In fine fashion, Ginny offered us a neat selection of modern-day San Francisco "wealth" to share with ALMANAC readers:

Thanks to Roxanne for the lead!

Little Italy Ristorante

4109 24th Street
821-1515
Call for hours (dinner only)
Reservations a must!

J.P. Gillen and his partner, attorney Jim Smith, own this attractive, active and noisy restaurant, which is named after New York's famed neighborhood and restaurant. We were taken here by close friends who know J.P. from his Connecticut days.

The smell of garlic, wine and spices waft through this small eatery, which has a semi-open kitchen. We adored the stuffed mushrooms, fried bread with cheese, a delectable shrimp marinara dish (stuffed with garlic) and more. Moderately priced. Mmm...

Wok Shop Cafe

1307 Sutter Street
(btwn. Franklin & Van Ness)
771-2142
Min. charge on home delivery
Open 7 days, lunch & dinner
No MSG, no credit cards

This rather bare-bones cafe is the answer to a longtime need. We have looked for many years for good, **hot**, home-delivered Chinese food.

The Wok Shop Cafe is conveniently located for eating before the Galaxy Theater's first showing (half price, you know). When eating at the cafe, the standout dish is Sizzling Jumbo Shrimp, a house dish at a modest $7.95. For home delivery, we normally order the $7.95 or $8.95 dinner. Each offers appetizer, soup, chicken, beef and rice with additions for three, four or five diners. Both dinners are divine for two people or more and will feed 3–4 people each, easily. If you call and ask them to mail you a menu, it includes a couple of free Cokes or Tsing Tao Beers, the former with minimum $10 order, the latter with $20 or more. The fortune cookies are thrown in free. A great meal, delivered hot and delicious.

SeniorNet

399 Arguello Blvd.
750-5030, call for information packet

This superb organization is dedicated to introducing seniors (age 55-and-over) to computer use and telecommunications. At various labs around the country (an IBM-clone learning center downtown and a Mac center at USF) young-at-heart men and women can learn basic terminology and word processing (through Microsoft Works), as well as how to trace a family tree, make original greeting cards, produce a newsletter and keep financial and tax records—all on computer. Become a member and get various discounts, from computers to Microsoft Works to Egghead Software—and a deal for America Online, where seniors can "talk" to others via computer modem.

—*Editor* Ginny Kolmar

1906 Earthquake Shacks

16,448 people lived in these one-room cabins in the years 1906–1908. Camps of shacks were set up in many prominent SF town squares and park sites. The shacks consisted of four redwood walls, a pitched roof, a fir floor, a door and two windows. Rent was $2/month.

Union carpenters constructed the shacks at combined cost of $870,479.81. A priority plan dictated who got a shack and who stayed in their tent, a friend's cellar or out of town. Shack dwellers had to bring their own heat stove and insulation. Sorry, no bath!

Of the 5,610 refugee shacks built in the wake of the 1906 earthquake, only twenty-three known (certified) 1906 shacks remain in San Francisco. From 1982-1992 *The Society for the Preservation and Appreciation of San Francisco Refugee Shacks* worked to preserve these valuable City relics. If you know of a "lost" shack or would like to receive or offer shack information, call historian Jane Cryan, (415) 759-6429.

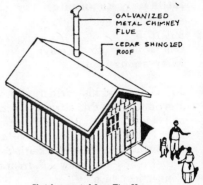

GALVANIZED METAL CHIMNEY FLUE

CEDAR SHINGLED ROOF

Sketch excerpted from *Tiny Houses*,
Lester Walker, AIA, Overlook Press, 1986

Refugee Shacks in SF, Today

- 1227 24th Avenue—Four Shacks, Sunset (Declared SF Landmark #171)
- 4329-31 Kirkham Street—Four Shacks, Sunset
- 165 Parker Avenue—Two Shacks, Richmond
- 349 27th Avenue—Three Shacks, Richmond (Scheduled for demolition)
- 254 Montana Street—One Shack, Ingleside
- 164 Bocana Street—One Shack, Bernal Heights
- 300 Cumberland St.—Three Shacks, Noe Valley
- 20 Newman Street—Two Shacks, Holly Park
- 211 Mullen Avenue—One Shack, Bernal Heights
- US Army Presidio Museum—Two Shacks

Jane Cryan, energetic guardian of the refugee shacks and founder of the [shack preservation] Society, now officially closed, has written a book about the 1906 refugee shack saga. *Hope Chest: A History of One of the Most Magnificent Charities of All Time*, will be available in 1993, a story of ordinary people in extraordinary times. Written in an entertaining but scholarly style, *Hope Chest* illuminates the lives of the shack dwellers and their battles against hunger, cold, civic graft and chaotic living conditions through first person accounts, maps and rare photographs. In our next ALMANAC issue we will offer a full feature review...

The San Remo Restaurant

Visit the San Remo Restaurant soon for supper fun and fare that is a reminder of the spirit of a rebuilding San Francisco following the 1906 earthquake. Already quite popular with locals and visitors, this turn-of-the-century restaurant and bar reopened under the historic hotel's excellent management in Summer 1992. The dinner menu features the foods one might have ordered in that day, including Italian, Chinese and homemade American dishes. Look for the piano, the charming pressed-tin ceilings and the elegant mahogany bar, shipped around Cape Horn. A favorite site for banquets, parties and weddings, this fun "bistro" can accommodate special celebrations attended by more than 100 guests. Dinner served Tuesday-Sunday. Near Fisherman's Wharf/North Beach at 2237 Mason Street. Call 673-9090. (See San Remo Hotel: *Room at the Inn.*)

The San Remo Hotel (originally called the New California Hotel) was built in 1906, immediately following the April earthquake, to answer the desperate need for post-quake housing. A.P. Giannini, founder of the Bank of America, was instrumental in helping to build the hotel. With its proximity to the Wharf and the Embarcadero, it became a home-away-from-home for hard-working merchant seamen and waterfront workers.

Seismic House Tour with Engineer Tony DeMascole

Is your 100-year-old Victorian or wood-frame building going to survive "The Big One?" Well-respected San Francisco structural engineer Anthony DeMascole gives invaluable home seismic safety tips in Owner-Builder Center's 30-minute video, *Earthquake: Home Safe Home.*

The tape explains how earthquakes can destroy wood-frame houses and how to do basic retrofitting tasks that strengthen older homes. The tape is available for $19.95 at OBC. An 80-page OBC book, *Introduction to Earthquake Retrofitting,* is available for $9.95. It makes a great companion reference.

Call the Owner-Builder Center at (510) 848-6860. (Tony also offers an OBC class on this subject. Ask to receive a class schedule. Recommended.)

How to Cut Your Water Use in Half

Randall Harrison, a long-time San Franciscan, wrote this darling little guide in 1977; it is still timely. Fifty pages of great water-saving ideas for just $4.00 ppd. Send payment to The Communication Press, Box 22541, Sunset Station, SF 94122. Randall's hilarious sketches and doodles make this book a special treat!

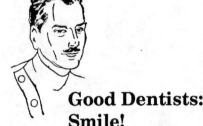

Good Dentists: Smile!

We are often asked by folks to recommend a good dentist in The City. We can recommend these offices with great pleasure.

Dr. Hilda Noguiero is located at 2674 Ocean Avenue. She and her husband, Dr. Kevin Burns, offer excellent general dentistry for both adults and children, 731-5104.

For root canal work, we suggest Dr. Fred Dias at 345 West Portal Avenue, 661-1595. Remarkably painless and quick.

For periodontal/gum check-ups and surgery, etc., call Dr. Paul Speert's office at 2355 Ocean Avenue, 333-1173.

A timely investment in your teeth is always rewarded with better health and a brighter smile.

Desktop Publishing in The Haight–Epicenter

1685 Haight Street (by Cole St.)
Located inside Copy Central
(formerly Carbon Alternative)
863-4304

Joel Pomerantz opened Epicenter Desktop in 1992, providing the Haight with a sorely needed desktop publishing business. Three Apple Macintoshes are available; each is loaded with standard word processing programs, graphics and paint programs and more. Usage is self-service, at affordable hourly rates. Copy Central's photocopying, color copying and binding services are nearby.

Epicenter Desktop was created to help Joel get another long-planned project off the ground: the Event Planning Information Center (EPICENTER). Joel plans to provide a free weekly telephone calendar to help keep the community abreast of the many activist events, special programs and arts happenings that make SF such an exciting place to live. To find out how your group can use this service, or to offer your resources, call Joel at 221-8172, or reach him at Epicenter Desktop. Good luck, Joel!

The San Francisco Community Calendar

Rick Hauptman publishes this most informative SF monthly calendar. If your community group, political club or event organization wishes to get the word out, this is a good start, and listings are free. A year's subscription to the handy calendar is just $11.00. Send check to: *SF Community Calendar,* 1595 Noe Street #6, SF, CA 94131. Include your name, address, city, state and zip code. For further information, call 647-0549.

Local Modem: In our next issue we will begin an annual round-up of Bay Area computer bulletin boards for the many modem users among us. If you'd like to contribute such information, please contact the ALMANAC Editor at 1-800-352-5268. Listings will be free. Thanks! (No dating services, please.)

Fort Mason Center

Fort Mason was constructed between 1909–1914 to serve as a base for expanding Pacific maritime operations following the Spanish-American War. When WWII began, Fort Mason served as the Pacific Port of Embarcation; 1½ million troops and 23 million tons of cargo were shipped out to the Pacific.

Today, Fort Mason is a part of the Golden Gate National Recreation Area (GGNRA), the largest urban park in the US. Fifty organizations call Fort Mason home. Call GGNRA at 556-0560.

Building A
City Celebration, Inc. 474-3914
Fort Mason Foundation, 441-5706
Greens Restaurant, 771-6222
Perception Gallery, 388-4331
SF Craft & Folk Art Museum, 775-0990
Plowshares Coffeehouse, 441-8910
SFMMA Rental Gallery, 441-4777
Tassajara Bread Bakery, 771-6330

Building B
Arts Arbitration Services, 775-7715
California Tomorrow, 441-7631
City College Art Center, 561-1840
Cooks and Company, 673-4137
Earth Drama Lab, 441-4441
Life on the Water, 776-8999
Marin Exchange, 441-6600
Ploughshares Fund, 775-2244

Building C
The Book Bay Bookstore, 771-1076
California Lawyers for Arts, 775-7200
Environ. Travel Companions, 474-7662

Friends of the River, 771-0400
The Fund for Animals, 474-4020
Make-A-Circus, 776-8477
Museo Italo Americano, 673-2200
Nat. Ctr. for Financial Ed., 567-5290
Performing Arts Workshop, 673-2634
SF African American Society, 441-0640
SF Children's Art Center, 771-0292
Young Performers' Theatre, 346-5550

Building D
Blue Bear School of Music, 673-3600
Friends of the Public Library, 771-3777
Magic Theatre, 441-8822
Media Alliance, 441-2557
Mexican Museum, 441-0404
National Poetry Association, 776-6602
Western Public Radio, 771-1161

Building E
Associates Shaw Library, 556-9870
Earth Island Institute, 921-3140
Lifeline Marine Research, 775-6497
Marine Mammal Fund, 775-4636
Oceanic Society Expeditions, 441-1106
Resource Renewal Institute, 775-2177
Sailing Education Adventures, 775-8779
SF Maritime National Park, 556-3002
J. Porter Shaw Library, 556-9870

Pier 1
BayKeeper, 567-4401
SS Jeremiah O'Brien Office, 441-3101

Pier 2
Bayfront Gallery, 441-5706
Cowell Theatre, 441-5706
Herbst Pavilion, 441-5706

Pier 3
Festival Pavilion, 441-5706
SS Jeremiah O'Brien, 441-3101

Fort Mason Center

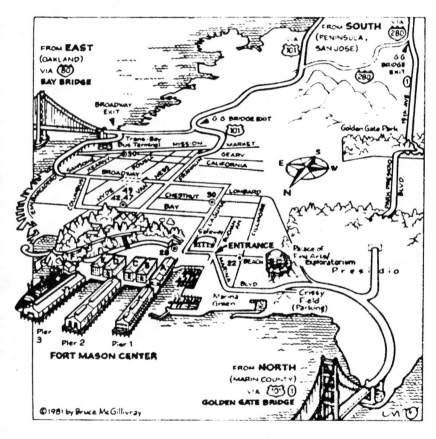

Pick up a copy of Fort Mason Center's monthly newsletter, *At the Park,* for a complete schedule of events and activities.

Gateway to the Park:
The Inner Sunset &
The Mid-Winter Fair

The Inner Sunset neighborhood's history is deeply rooted in the 1894 Mid-Winter Fair held at Golden Gate Park. This earliest of SF's world's fairs was the first of its type that was *not* funded by a city, state or national government. Contributions were accepted from private citizens to raise the fair in hopes of kick-starting a bad local and national economy. Much of the fair's ornamentation was brought to SF from the 1892 Chicago World's Fair after it closed. The "new" Inner Sunset neighborhood served as the Park's southern entrance, much the same as it does today.

The Fair was held from January to July 1894, and featured a "Sunny California" theme, demonstrating the state's year-round growing seasons. Sixty acres of Golden Gate Park were transformed, in only five months, into a World's Fair replete with grand expositions and fancy carnival rides.

The Electric Tower, similiar in design to the Eiffel Tower, was 632-feet-high and was lit by 8,000 new electric lamps!

THE ALMANAC looks forward to presenting an illustrated feature celebrating the Mid-Winter Fair Centennial in 1994.

The Electric Tower was 632 feet tall and contained 8,000 lamps.

Bavarian Apple Torte from *The Treasure Island Cookbook*

Crust:
½ Cup Butter
¼ Cup Sugar
¼ tsp. Vanilla
1 Cup Flour

Cream butter with sugar, add vanilla and flour. Spread onto bottom and sides of 9" round pan.

Filling:
8 Ounces Cream Cheese
¼ Cup Sugar
1 Egg
½ tsp. Vanilla

Apple Topping:
¼ Cup Sugar
¼ tsp. Cinnamon
4 Cups thinly sliced and peeled
Golden Delicious Apples

Combine softened cream cheese and sugar and mix well. Blend in egg and vanilla and pour into pastry-lined pan.

Combine sugar and cinnamon and toss over apples. Spoon this mixture over cream cheese. Bake at 450° for 10 minutes, reduce heat to 400° for 25 minutes. Cool before removing from pan. This cake is very good cold, with or without whipping cream. Serves 8–10. Enjoy!

This delicious torte recipe was contributed by Joy Westphal to a cookbook being prepared as a fundraiser for The Treasure Island Museum. Joy has made a home on Naval bases all over the U.S. and Japan, but notes, "When I prepare this torte, my heart returns to my hometown in Wisconsin, and my beloved grandmother."

ALMANAC readers who would like to submit a recipe to *The Treasure Island Cookbook* are welcome to do so. Include a few words about what makes your recipe special to you. Send it to: Treasure Island Museum Association, Cookbook Editor, Building 1 Treasure Island, SF, CA 94130. When the book is ready (1993-ish) notices will be sent to all contributors. Great gift!

Skulls on the Range:

Traveling Skull Merchant Jim Pochinchuk

Jim Pochinchuk and partner Joe Whalen are in the skull business: cow skulls, that is. Pochinchuk sells a selection of beautifully prepared cow, horse, deer and Angora ram skulls from his trail-beaten Chevrolet van to individual buyers, wholesalers, decorators and restaurants throughout SF and the Bay Area.

Sales are expanding. Jim's skulls are sold in local Southwestern decor shops around the Bay, including Southwest Images and Coyote. Retail sales from his modern-day Conestoga wagon (his van) are brisk, too. Popular locations include Haight Street, the Financial District and roadside locations in Sacramento. Recently Chevy's Restaurants bought over fifty of these symbols of the cycle of life, and "Some rock 'n' roll shops sell the skulls," Jim says. "Death rockers love the stuff!"

Most folks purchase the skulls for their stark natural beauty. The expanding interest in early Southwestern decor knows no limit. "I don't think it's a style of interior design that has really begun to be realized," Jim offers. "The look is so graceful."

How does Jim get his merchandise? He often saddles up and rides into the Central Valley and Nevada to purchase skulls from ranchers and farmers who set them aside for him. (He buys only skulls from reputable ranchers and will not purchase the bones from animals killed by hunters.) Jim then dries the skulls on the roof of his Sacramento apartment after carefully boiling the sun-bleached bones. "Sometimes the neighbors think I'm a Satanic skull worshipper," he quips. Jim is actually one of the sweetest and gentlest entrepreneurs you could ever meet. One retailer comments, "He has a good product, he's a nice young man to work with and his prices are fair. He delivers what he promises, too."

Call Jim if you'd like to see his collection of Desert Originals, (415) 330-5396. He can visit your shop or tell you where you can find him out on the range. Skulls generally range from $60–$500.

Do Not eAT:
Rave Jewelry

Rob Prideaux, along with Dina Stark and Ted Stachura, have created a "Rave" jewelry line called Do Not eAT. The group got its break when the dance-all-night Rave haunt Toon Town allowed Do Not eAT to open a retail outlet in its club at 165 King Street, South of Market.

Rob's energetic pendants and earrings are individually crafted from a clay-like plastic, featuring many of the leading Rave dance-hall icons in wild day-glo pink, blue, orange and yellow. His rockets, planets and coffee cups use bright chrome and galvanized attachments and chains. (Earrings are equipped with sterling silver hangers.)

You can ask for Do Not eAT jewelry at Ameba (1732 Haight Street, 750-9368) and at Futura (2374 Telegraph Ave., Berkeley (510) 843-3037), as well as at shops in San Jose, Los Angeles and Melrose.

Sales Rep. Dina would be pleased to speak to anyone interested in retailing the vivid, fun and futuristic jewelry. Call (415) 885-4960. A color catalogue is available to retailers. Rave on...

Superiority through Constant Motion

Do Not eAT jewelry is available at Toon Town and Ameba on Haight Street, or call (415) 885-4960 for other locations.

ALMANAC White Elephant

SF's Finest Thrift Shops, Collectibles and 'Round-Again Fashions

Antiques in the Rough

1767 Waller Street (by Stanyan)
221-0194
Thurs. & Fri. Noon - 5 p.m.
Sat. & Sun. 9 a.m. - 5:30 p.m.

This fine shop, just a block off Haight Street by Stanyan, has served the neighborhood need for clocks, furniture and art-ish items since 1963. Many of the original Haight Street hipsters were their customers then and still return today.

Armoires, chairs, tables, phonographs and music boxes are popular. If you like Victorian looks, this place will tantalize you. Please *do* ask for help with things with moving parts. The staff is friendly, casual, very cooperative and well-informed.

The selection is fun and inspires curiosity and creativity. For those who are new to the world of antiques, there are great pieces available at sometimes stunningly inexpensive prices. Cash, check (with ID) and all credit cards accepted.

When you walk by, observe the teddy bears in the window. They change what they are doing every fortnight.

National Council of Jewish Women

The National Council of Jewish Women was founded in 1893. Its volunteer members are dedicated to serving the local home community, the nation and Israel through advocacy and direct services. The San Francisco Section supports numerous beneficial local programs. If you can help, contact NCJW, which is in turn helps these and other programs in The City:

WICS–Women in Community Service working together to help young women help themselves in today's job market.

Bargain Mart–The popular Divisadero Street thrift shop whose profits help make SF Section NCJW services possible.

Menorah Mart–A non-profit Jewish grocery at a Jewish senior residence, Menorah Park.

Library Project–Adults working with children in SF school libraries.

Pathways to English–A tutorial program in conjunction with the SF School Volunteers, teaching reading and language skills to children and young adults.

Children's Drama Service–A traveling theatre group that performs for disabled children in special schools in the Bay Area.

These are just some of the ways you can help as a NCJW member or volunteer. Call 346-4600.

Bear-ly New

UC Medical Hospital Auxiliary
1752 Fillmore Street
(btwn. Sutter & Post)
921-2789
Mon.-Sat. 10 a.m. - 5 p.m.

This especially delightful Fillmore Street thrift store benefits the UC Medical Center. Look for great buys on designer labels for ladies, nicer men's clothes and a great housewares and gift collection in this cozy little store.

This shop is kept neat as a pin, and may be the most "romantic" in this ALMANAC. Manager Estelle Blair encourages donations, but suggests you call ahead, as shop space is limited. Estelle and her staff's hard work and a long list of regular shoppers and contributors make Bear-ly New a must for thrifters looking for treasures and rare finds.

The shop opened in 1979 at 25th & Clement and moved into its present location in 1980. No layaways! First come, first served, get it while you can! Cash or checks accepted.

The Bottom Drawer

St. Vincent de Paul Church
2810 Pierce Street (at Green)
776-1165
Tues., Thurs., Sat. 10 a.m. - 3 p.m.

Run by St. Vincent de Paul Catholic Church's Ladies Auxiliary, The Bottom Drawer began 17 years ago in one room. Now it fills the entire first floor of the convent. It is a rare treat to find kitchen items displayed in a "real" kitchen.

One of The City's favorite thrift shops, The Bottom Drawer has quite a star-studded list of regular shoppers.

There are sales often, including "bag sales" in late May or early June, before closing shop for the summer.

Cash or checks, no bargaining, no layaway and all sales final. The stock moves fast, so shop often. The shop prides itself on offering fresh merchandise every day. Convenient to Union St./North Beach/Masonic bus routes 22, 41 and 43.

Donations benefit the church's youth sports program. Bring a lunch, sit outside and see with your own eyes why the well-to-do favor Pacific Heights. *The Bottom Drawer is a great way to spend a rainy afternoon, too!*

Cathedral School Shop

Cathedral School for Boys
1036 Hyde Street
(at California Street—CALA)
776-6630
Tues.-Sat. 10 a.m. - 5 p.m.

This delightful Nob Hill thrift shop has that certain something that makes it unique. Perhaps it's the adorable awning-shaded storefront, or maybe it's the lace and needlepoint feeling of the place. Perhaps it's the clanging of the cable car at the corner.

Cathedral School Shop is a classic little shop without pretense. The shop caters to families and young professionals and features quality clothing and children's items and toys. Collectibles pass through; look for silent auctions on special shop treasures, too.

This shop, a 25-year resident of the neighborhood, provides a scholarship fund for the Cathedral School for Boys. Popular Manager Bonnie Germain, who relocated to the hills of Montana for awhile, has returned. She manages a very friendly staff, including Wendy Boyce and Don Brady. Volunteers Freddie Lewin and Charlotte Durkee (who turns 92 this year) and a long list of wonderful school parents keep this little thrift shop buzzing!

Community Thrift Store

The Tavern Guild
625 Valencia Street (btwn. 17th & 18th)
861-4910
Daily 10 a.m. - 6 p.m.

Community Thrift Store is one of SF's most popular non-profit thrift stores and is well-supported by the gay community. This shop earmarks your donation to one of over 180 community programs, with 75 percent of proceeds going to dozens of AIDS-related programs throughout The City.

Decorators, designers and dealers are frequent shoppers here. A huge bric-a-brac section attracts collectible hunters. There is a large furniture supply and a big selection of clothes, shoes and linens. A well-screened book and magazine thrift section is The City's largest and is always busy with browsers.

Donations can be dropped off during most of the day at the alley-door to the right of the building (enter from Mission Street—one-way alley).

Truck pick-ups are daily, but call at least one week ahead for scheduling. Look for the pink and blue storefront, which is a converted warehouse. Cash only. One of SF's best!

Hospice Community Thrift Shop

Hospice-by-the-Bay
1173 Sutter (btwn. Polk & Larkin)
673-3030 (Hospice 673-2020)
Weekdays 9 a.m. - 5 p.m.
Saturdays 9:30 a.m. - 5 p.m.

This busy thrift shop supports Hospice-by-the-Bay, a non-profit home and in-patient hospice that cares for people and their families during the late stages of terminal illness. Now four-years-old, the shop helps support hospice resources such as the new live-in care facility being built on Leland Avenue.

Great shop for small furniture, household items, bric-a-brac, collectibles and jewelry. Annual school drives net plenty of good kids' stuff, too. Colored tag sales run constantly, with special sales popping up. Layaways. Donations welcome. You may drop your donations off at the store, or call to schedule free pickup at your home.

Manager Gail Acevedo also urgently needs a few good, steady volunteers. Call Gail to join up. (The shop offers a 20% discount to volunteers.) Cash, MasterCard & Visa accepted.

Welcome to Judy Fischer, Gail's new Assistant Manager. Best to you, Judy!

Next-to-New Shop

The Junior League of SF
2226 Fillmore Street
(btwn. Clay & Sacramento)
567-1627
Mon.-Sat. 11 a.m. - 4 p.m.
Closed Sundays
Call for revised hours.

The Fillmore St. "Thrift Alley" owes a thank-you to store manager Lita Smith. Lita, who began as a Junior League volunteer some 23 years ago, not only manages this firmly established thrift store, but has also given a hand to several other shops just starting out.

Next-To-New brings designer labels and men's and women's fashions to the fore. The store also has a good selection of housewares and magazines.

Donations are encouraged; drop off donations before 3:30 p.m. Pick-ups are also possible.

Proceeds support the Junior League of S.F., a non-profit volunteer agency that promotes volunteerism. Cash and checks accepted. Closed August and over Christmas.

Recommended for better women's fashions and the young, eager staff.

NEXT - TO - NEW

The Junior League of San Francisco

The Next-To-New Shop gratefully accepts your tax deductible donations. Donations are welcomed from anyone. All donations are itemized and a tax deductible receipt is sent to the donor. In the event that you need to schedule a pick-up of your donations, please call The Next-To-New Shop. Feel free to stop in anytime.

Next-To-New Shop
2226 Fillmore Street
415-567-1627

Ocean Avenue Thrift Shop

1619 Ocean Avenue
(By City College,
btwn. Faxon & Capitol)
239-8766
Tues.-Sat. 10 a.m. - 4 p.m.

The Ocean Avenue Thrift Shop is one of The City's most colorful. Well managed by Ann-Mari Gettys, this neighborhood shop receives donations from neighborhood residents and Waldorf School parents and staff. All proceeds benefit The Waldorf School.

Look for clothing, costume jewelry, kitchen items and one of the best collections of "junk drawer" knick-knacks and collectibles around. Lots of books. Frequently kids' toys, books and clothing, too. Antiquey and vintage clothing items and hats pass through this shop, which is packed wall-to-wall with items.

Ann encourages donations of all items. Ocean Avenue Thrift Shop, by the way, is well-established in its location. It was a City of Hope fundraiser for almost twenty years, before Waldorf School bought the shop lock, stock and barrel, almost four years ago. It is a most popular place with the local residents, a sort of "town square" for the many neighbors.

One of SF's best thrift shops, with a fun, friendly manager who loves to bargain.

Presidio Thrift Store

The Presidio of San Francisco
Bldg. 204 (follow signs off of Presidio Drive to Thrift Store)
922-3384
Tues.-Thurs. 10 a.m. - 2 p.m.
(Also open first Sat./month)

Housed in a converted stable near the Presidio Headquarters, Presidio Thrift Shop offers on-the-go military personnel a place to consign their household goods. Proceeds are directed to a host of groups. Only persons with valid military ID may consign, but the public is warmly invited to come and shop.

Look for high-quality household items, sporting goods, records and tapes and tools. On the first Saturday of each month, the shop is open and a flea market is held out front. The Presidio Thrift Shop has operated to benefit both military and civilian San Franciscans since 1946. Great thrift prices!

Recommended City secret!

While you're there, be sure to visit *The Creative Cottage,* right next door, for a terrific assortment of very affordable craft and gift items. There are local cookbooks, kitchen crafts, handmade paper goods, toys, decorations and more.

Pine Street Collectibles

1467 Pine Street (off Polk)
885-2870
Tues.-Sat. 11 a.m. - 7 p.m.
Sun. 11 a.m. - 6 p.m.

This loft-like furniture and collectibles shop is the perfect solution for those who want unique furniture but don't have a lot of money.

Look for a very large selection of dressers, desks, mirrors, tables, chairs and other upbeat and useful furnishings. A recent visit revealed beautiful and quite affordable church pews, popular Asian items and some very entertaining wall pieces and paintings from many eras and nations.

A relaxed, sophisticated shop (note the owners' ongoing chess game), Pine Street Collectibles is a bright solution for those who have "champagne dreams" on a root-beer budget. Friendly owners Leon Monderer and Kin Wong do buy outright: call. All forms of payment are accepted. Delivery and pick-up are available via their own store truck.

A must-stop shop for colorful furniture pieces that show thought, taste and style. Nearby are many cafes and bookstores, so make a day of it!

St. Vincent de Paul Society

The St. Vincent de Paul Society was founded in Paris in 1833 by Frederic Ozanam. In July of 1885, the Society formed its San Francisco branch. During the Great Depression, they operated a center on Mission Street. The outpouring of goods and clothing was so great that they set up a thrift store to convert that surplus into much-needed dollars.

The Society not only serves Catholics but also involves people of all denominations, regardless of race or creed. It depends on concerned corporate and private support from those who want to assist the needy.

Programs include *Rosalie House*, a shelter for battered women and their families; the *Arlington Hotel*, a sober home for indigents; *Ozanam Center*, a multi-faceted resource center and other programs.

A new program for victims of battery will open soon, to be called *The Brennan House*. The shelter is named after Frank Brennan of the Seven Seas, a tireless advocate for alcoholics. Find out how you or your business can help.

Two San Francisco Thrift Shops

1519 Haight (near Ashbury)
863-3615
Weekdays 9:30 a.m. - 4:45 p.m.
Saturdays 9 a.m. - 4:45 p.m.
Sundays Noon - 5 p.m.

Main Facility
1745 Folsom (at 13th)
626-1515
Weekdays 9:30 a.m. - 4:45 p.m.
Saturdays 9 a.m. - 4:45 p.m.

The "Blue & White Circle" runs two highly recommended thrift stores in SF. Both offer good clothing, shoes, sweaters, coats and jackets and household goods; they are also excellent places to look for unique collectibles. The larger **Folsom St.** store has a large selection of furniture, tables and chairs. It also has a "thrift boutique," which offers finer items. Over at **Haight St.**, shop boss Helen Borja is popular with customers. Deliveries from the Folsom store on Mondays, Wednesdays and Fridays.

Donations can be delivered to either store, or call 626-1515 for planned weekday pick-up. Marin residents call 1-800-637-7837.

Special thanks to St. Vincent de Paul's hardworking Staff Director Richard Bright and crew for their tireless work in San Francisco.

Salvation Army

1509 Valencia Street (at Army)
695-8040
Mon., Wed., Fri. 9:30 a.m. - 9 p.m.
Tues., Thurs., Sat. 9:30 a.m. - 6 p.m.

1185 Sutter (at Polk)
771-3818
Mon.-Sat. 9 a.m. - 5 p.m.
(Thurs. to 7 p.m.)

Call 695-8000 for donations pick-up in San Francisco.

The Salvation Army is a branch of the Christian church. It was founded in England in 1865 and came to San Francisco in 1882. Perhaps the best-known thrift merchant, they are known for their red-shielded trucks, the jingle of bells at Christmas and, of course, their thrift shops.

The large central store at **Valencia** offers a selection of clothing that stretches the length of a football field; they also have a large selection of shoes and accessories. This is no place for thrift lightweights! Good selection of bikes, appliances, TV's and stereos, stoves, heaters, lamps and furniture. While you're there, check "The Inn Shoppe," a small boutique that carries wool and leather items and collectibles. The smaller shop at **Sutter Street**, downtown, carries a wide selection of furniture, kitchen stuff and appliances.

Salvation Army projects include the shelter for the homeless on Eddy Street; *Harbor Light Alcoholic Services*; *The Pinehurst Lodge*, a home for women in crisis and a 600-acre working ranch in Healdsburg. Needs of seniors are met through various programs, including the *Silvercrest Residence*, home to 260 people. They also operate a facility at Army and Valencia where 115 men receive housing, meals, health care and counseling.

China Hunt

If you're searching for replacement pieces for missing or discontinued China settings, send a self-addressed stamped envelope marked *China List* to THE SAN FRANCISCO ALMANAC, 1657 Waller Street #A, SF, CA 94117-2811. The list was compiled by Gump's, a famous China merchant since 1861, and features English China, Franciscan, German/Bavarian, Haviland China, Lenox, Mikasa, Minton and others. Allow one week for receipt of the handy list of 20 dealers of discontinued China in the US.

Still Life

515 Frederick Street
(by Stanyan/Kezar Stadium)
759-1234
Everyday Noon - 5 p.m.
(Saturday Opens at 10 a.m.)

Owner Ron Lehmer has been here since "The Summer of Love," just two blocks from Haight Street. If you're after finished or unfinished bookshelves, dressers, armoires and classic 20th Century furniture items, get over to Still Life.

Ron likes to work within a customer's budget to develop a long-lasting buyer/seller friendship. He'll offer suggestions if he doesn't have an item in stock or perhaps he'll make it himself. Affordable quality refinishing is offered, too.

The name Still Life is very Ron-esque. It represents the usual meaning of a painting in repose and also means "it's still got life left in it." Shop personnel Chase and Alex are skilled, helpful and quite knowledgeable, too.

Still Life has always been a favorite for its new unfinished pine and oak bookshelves. Recently, Ron has added a versatile line of quite affordable "Victorian" trim shelves with adjustable decks, oversize dowry trunks and other built-to-spec pieces for quality home or office furnishings. Visit soon.

The Third Hand Store

1839 Divisadero Street
567-7332
Mon.-Sat. Noon - 6 p.m.

The Third Hand Store, which opened in 1967, was the very first vintage shop in California. As they say, quality lasts!

Vintage, it seems, began in Portland, Oregon, and then almost simultaneously here. Owners Charles and Jean Stewart saw a chance to serve hippies looking for period fashions for day-to-day use.

The Third Hand Store offers finer vintage clothing and accessories that fit to a T. Items include tuxedos, evening gowns, hats, shoes and a full range of sparkling accoutrements, all ready-to-wear and in great shape. A sizeable costume and ethnic jewelry collection rounds it out.

Shopkeepers Joseph and Suzanne, both knowledgeable fashion collectors, are friendly, most helpful and fun. They have rented clothing for films and have even outfitted entire period wedding parties. Perfume spokeswoman and *Umbrellas of Cherbourg* star Catherine Deneuve frequents this shop, among others, when in SF on business.

Checks, MasterCard, Visa and American Express accepted. Great prices!

Wasteland

1660 Haight (at Belvedere)
863-3150
Mon.-Fri. 11 a.m. - 6 p.m.
Sat. 11 a.m. - 7 p.m.
Sun. Noon - 6 p.m.

Wasteland is a popular used-clothing and jewelry market that is housed in a cavernous 1918 silent-movie palace. This young Berkeley clothing outfit brought its proven East Bay model to SF just two years ago with confidence and sureness. Since then, this low-pain buy, sell and swap operation has proved immensely popular with SF's leading-edge fashion crowd.

The store has very reasonable pricing in men's and women's quality clothing and accessories. "Victorian" fashions are popular, and guess what, kids, bell-bottoms are back! The large '60s selection moves quickly. Many "Rave" items are available, also. Visa, MasterCard and checks accepted.

Wasteland is always busy, but avoid weekends if you can. Buyers on hand Noon - 4 p.m. daily.

Their collectibles and furniture gallery has really come around and they buy these items, too. Wasteland has relocated the Berkeley store to a great new shop at 2398 Telegraph Avenue. For directions from SF, call (510) 843-6711.

The White Elephant & The Hungry Bulldog

For our first two years, we offered reviews to well over 100 shops at no charge. As publication costs mounted, we were unable to keep offering every good thrift, collectible and vintage shop in The City complete reviews. (Nine California thrift/collectible guides have started and failed for lack of ad revenue since we published our first issue in 1990.) We lost a lot of sleep over this, and finally asked: What would our readers suggest? We chose to request a small payment for a full ALMANAC White Elephant review and *Almanac News* services for the entire year. (This would help "feed the bulldog.") We have included full-length reviews of those shops that supported us, and mini-reviews for the others. We are *very* thankful to our most special ALMANAC sponsors and encourage you to visit their great shops. To the rest, we extend a warm invitation to tell our fine readers more about your store in the next ALMANAC series.
Thanks—WB

PS: We still have 50 copies of our first "Thrift Shop Almanac," offering full reviews of 80 shops. If you'd like one, send us $7.00 ppd. Collectors' items? We hope so!

More Shops...

Cookin' at 339 Divisadero (861-1854) carries a very large collection of pre-owned cooking and serving items and over 600 cookbooks. *Next-to-New, Community Thrift Store, Cathedral School Shop* and *The Salvation Army* (two shops) are also good bets for finding older kitchen items just like those we remember from childhood supper tables.

A-One Hubcaps at 528 Divisadero (431-0525) stocks 50,000 auto wheel covers, specializing in Ford and Chrysler.

The Salvation Army offers two stores reviewed in this ALMANAC. The larger Valencia street store offers bicycles, appliances and stoves, heaters and the like. There are daily appliance auctions at 9 a.m. across the street at The Salvation Army's loading dock/alley area, but we haven't had a chance to see these. Let us know...

St. Vincent de Paul Society's Folsom Street store offers a funky annex shop that might just be the place to look for that odd who-jam-it that the handyperson can never find in the junk drawer! St. Vincent de Paul's smaller Haight Street store gets more popular for shopping and donations every day!

Savers and Thrift Town are SF's largest for-profit department second-hand stores, located at 2840 Geneva (468-0646) and 2101 Mission Street (861-1132). Both offer vast selections of thrift household items, second-hand clothing and furniture and collectibles.

Bear-ly New at 1752 Fillmore Street surprises you often with great collectible and fashion deals. Shop often. Manager Estelle Blair and her helpful staff keep the new stock coming to keep the faithful customers coming and to benefit UC Medical Hospital. Highly recommended for surprises!

Next-to-New carries designer fashions to keep you at your sharpest! Manager Lita Smith runs an energetic thrift shop sponsored by The Junior League. The Pacific Heights crowd shops it up here. Recently Next-to-New billboards could be seen flashing by on Muni buses! Serious business here!

For collectibles, *Cathedral School Shop*, George Tabak's The Attic: Treasures of Yesteryear at 2445-2453 Taraval Street (661-DOLL), The Attic Shop at

1040 Hyde Street (474-3498) and Lorraine Choy's delightful Sweet Lorraine at 2036 Polk Street (474-7861) are definitely worth a visit. If you're a fan of the once wild, wild west, visit One-Eyed Jacks at 1645 Market Street at Brady Alley. Here you'll find a brand new shop featuring the boots, furniture, rugs, bones and other accoutrements featured in all our favorite Hollywood oaters. Auctions, too. Call.

After lamps or other small furniture items? No Name Collectibles at 603 Valencia Street (864-5743) is a small, cozy shop, located right next door to *Community Thrift Store*. No Name offers custom search services for hard-to-find items, furniture refinishing and will keep an eye out for that special item you're looking for. True Legends at 568 Haight Street (861-1130) is a shop straight from the pages of an antique Sears & Roebuck catalogue and carries a nice collection of older but not too-antiquey toys, lamps and tabletop pieces from many eras. *Antiques in the Rough* has great style pieces, too.

Pine Street Collectibles is highly recommended for neat wall pieces and small furniture items from all eras and is a great place to begin when looking for apartment items of many styles and eras. *Antiques in the Rough* is a well-known neighborhood shop for those who are looking for stylish and remarkably affordable antique furniture, amusement pieces and clocks.

Also try Sweet Home Antiques at 2001 Clement (387-2661) for medium to high-ticket collectible furniture and settings.

Don't forget *The Bargain Mart*, Big John's Misc. at 654 Fillmore Street by Alamo Square (861-6327), *Cathedral School Shop*, Kernan's Moving and Storage at 819 Valencia at 19th Street (647-9300), and, for more furniture choices than you would ever imagine, Cottrell's Moving & Storage at 150 Valencia Street (by Market, 431-1000). Cottrell's has carried hundreds of beds, dressers and armoires since 1905.

Not enough can be said about the fine pieces and prices at Ron Lehmer's popular neighborhood furniture and bookshelves store *Still Life* at 515 Frederick Street near Haight Street, by New Kezar Stadium. If you're after bookshelves, this is the spot. Great for affordable, fun furniture!

Fillmore Street remains a favorite destination for thrifters looking for collectibles or fashions. Victorian House Thrift Shop at 2318 Fillmore, Repeat Performance at 2223 Fillmore and Seconds-to-Go at 2252 Fillmore are just a few of the reasons. Also check Crossroads Trading Company at 1901 Fillmore, and always take in *Bear-ly New* (1752 Fillmore) and *Next-to-New*, 2226 Fillmore, two of Fillmore Street and The City's very best non-profit shops. Don't skip The Street Shop, too, a quaint little shop at 2011 Divisadero

Street (931-4382) just four blocks from Fillmore Street, close to *The Bargain Mart* and *The Third Hand Store*.

Modernology at 572 Hayes Street (863-2514) offers chairs for collectors and a unique "art"-ifacts gallery in swinging Hayes Valley. The shop now features a grand piano from The Fairmont Hotel for your listening enjoyment.

Rainbow's End Thrift Store is fun, located at 621 Divisadero Street (921-0216). Look for hats, small furniture items and funky knick-knacks and collectibles. Mary's Attic is another popular neighborhood shop at 2031 Irving Street in The Sunset (665-2950) particularly good for family clothing and shoes.

Hospice Community Thrift Shop at 1173 Sutter Street (673-3030) is one of SF's fastest growing thrift shops and benefits Hospice-by-the-Bay. Town School Clothes Closet at 3225 Sacramento Street (928-8019) is a thrift shop that benefits The Town School. If you're looking for art/industrial items such as old lamps, parts for anything mechanical, cameras and projectors, GI items and electronic hardware try Purple Heart Thrift Store at 1855 Mission Street (621-2581).

For collectible or vintage fashions, visit Spellbound at 1670 Haight Street (863-4930), La Rosa at 1711 Haight Street (two shops—668-3744), Departures from the Past at 2028 Fillmore Street (885-3377), Mary's Exchange at 24th Street and Castro in Noe Valley and Felino's at 3162 16th Street in The Mission (863-5706). If you are after 1940s fashions, Always and Forever at 3789 24th Street (285-7174) has been a popular Noe Valley neighborhood shop for these items since 1983.

The Third Hand Store at 1839 Divisadero Street (567-7332) is California's original vintage shop (since 1967) and offers a remarkably affordable and very fine collection of fashions and accessories from all eras. Recommended.

For more contemporary fashions, take a fun trip to Noe Valley and see Taren Saperienza's One More Time at 4156 24th Street, offering a bright, organized consignment fashion shop with lovely window decorations!

Wasteland has re-located their original Berkeley store to 2398 Telegraph Avenue. The new store is really sharp! The popular Haight Street store does a tremendous buy-sell-swap business in fashions from all eras, and is becoming a major collectibles buy and sell shop.

Watch for a book called "Tophats to Toasters" to be published by Heyday Books in Fall 1992, to offer listings of Bay Area second-hand shops and more.

Flea Markets Around The Bay

Thou know'st that all my fortunes are at sea; Neither have I money nor commodity to raise a present sum. Thereforth I go forth; Try what my credit can in Venice do.

The Merchant of Venice, W. Shakespeare

San Francisco

City of Hope/Fort Mason

World's Largest Garage Sale and Flea Market

SF's biggest once-a-year market at Fort Mason Center (held each Fall) offers hundreds of venders selling everything from soup-to-nuts. Call 391-6448 for information on this hospital fundraiser.

The Presidio Thrift Shop

The first Saturday of the month a fun and relaxed market is held in the Presidio Thrift Store parking lot. Call the thrift shop for info. (*See review.*)

St. Anthony's distributes clothing and household items free to homeless and low-income families and individuals who need such assistance. The center has a special demand for large men's and kids' clothing. To arrange pick-ups within SF, call at least a week in advance at 241-8300 (receipts).

The North Bay

Marin City Flea Market
147 Donohue, Marin City (off 101)
Weekends 331-6752
Weekdays 332-1441
Sat. 6 a.m. - 4 p.m.
Sun. 5 a.m. - 4 p.m.
Vender Fee: Car $20.00, Truck $30.00
No fee for market admission.

(This market may be moving soon. The lot the market currently occupies has been sold to a developer. Call before driving out to Marin.)

Midgley's Country Flea Market
2200 Gravenstein Hwy. S.
Sebastapol (off 101)
(707) 823-7874
Sat.-Sun. 6:30 a.m. - 4:30 p.m.
Vender Fee: Space $10.00, Shaded Space $13.00. Vender space includes 4 ft. by 8 ft. table.

Napa-Vallejo Flea Market & Auction
Kelly Road (off Hwy. 29)
226-8862
Sun. 6 a.m. - 5 p.m.
Call for vender fees.

The South Bay

Berryessa/San Jose Flea Market
12000 Berryessa Road,
between I-680 & 101
(408) 453-1110
Wed.-Sun. Dawn to Dusk, Year-Round
Vender Fee: Wed. $15.00, Thurs.-Fri. $10.00, Sat.-Sun $25.00.
No admission fee
Parking available, $3.00

DeAnza College
21250 Stevens Creek Blvd., Cupertino
(408) 864-8946
First Saturday Each Month
8 a.m. - 4 p.m.
Vender Fee: Single Space $14.00,
Double Space $30.00
Parking $1.00

Geneva Drive-In Flea Market
607 Carter, Daly City
(near Cow Palace)
587-0515
Sat.-Sun. 7 a.m. - 4 p.m.
Vender Fees: Sat. $10.00, Sun. $15.00
Small admission fee

Lake Merced/Doegler Center
101 Lake Merced Blvd., Daly City
991-8012
Second Sunday Each Month,
8 a.m. - 3 p.m.
Markets June-November
Vender Fee: $15.00
(10 ft. by 15 ft. space, table)
Free admission. (This is a great little market. Recommended fun.)

The East Bay

Alameda Penny Market
Island Auto Movie
off of Atlantic Ave., Alameda
(510) 522-7206
Sat.-Sun. 7 a.m. - 4:30 p.m.
Vender Fee: $10.00–$12.00/day
50¢ admission fee

Berkeley Flea Market
Ashby BART Station,
MLK Jr. Way & Ashby
(510) 644-0744
Sat-Sun. 8 a.m. - 7:30 p.m.
Vender Fee: $11.00/Day *(Advance payment is usually necessary as market is very popular. Call well ahead.)*

Chabot College Market/Hayward
25555 Hesperian Blvd.
(510) 786-6918
Third Saturday of Month,
8 a.m. - 4 p.m.
Vender Fee: $12.00–$15.00
No admission fee

Coliseum Swap Meet
Oakland Drive-In, 5401 Coliseum Way
(510) 534-0325
Thurs., Fri., Sat., Sun. 6:30 a.m. - 4 p.m.
Vender Fee: $7.50–$15.00
Small admission fee

Concord Bi-Annual Flea Market
Spring & Fall/ Call for Dates
(510) 798-6800
Vender Fee: $15.00
Small admission fee

Niles Antique Flea Market
Niles Business District, Fremont
(510) 792-8023
Last Sunday in August, 7 a.m. - 4 p.m.
Call to verify event schedule.
Vender Fee: $75.00

Norcal Swap Meet/Laney College
Seventh & Fallon, Oakland
(510) 769-7266
Sat.-Sun. 7 a.m. - 4 p.m.
Vender Fee: $6.00–$8.00
Free admission

Ohlone College Super Flea Market
43600 Mission Blvd., Fremont
(510) 659-6215
Second Saturday of each month,
7 a.m. - 4:30 p.m.
Vender Fee: $12.00
Free admission

Piedmont Avenue Flea Market
Piedmont & Yosemite, Oakland
(510) 655-5839
Sat.-Sun. 8 a.m. - 4 p.m.
Vender Fee: $15.00
Free admission

Solano Drive-In Market/Concord
Solano Way & Hwy. 4
(510) 543-3886
Sat. 7 a.m. - 4 p.m. Call for vender fees.

BOOKS

We began the magazine and bookseller feature in 1991, reviewing only the major *magazine* sellers in The City. We have included many *book*sellers this time, and will greatly expand our coverage of new and used booksellers in our next issue. We encourage booksellers to please call or write. Too many bookstores?! What a town!

A Clean Well-Lighted Place for Books

601 Van Ness Avenue
(Opera Plaza)
441-6670
Sun.-Thurs. 10 a.m. - 11 p.m.
Fri.-Sat. 10 a.m. - Midnight

A Clean Well-Lighted Place offers very good magazine racks and a great new book selection. Periodicals include trade journals, popular titles, literary publications and vogues. There is some emphasis on design, art and architecture and some small press output. The shop is open late every night, too.

The store's name was borrowed from *A Clean Well-Lighted Place,* a fine short story written by Ernest Hemingway in Paris in the 1930s. At the time he was making a living selling stories to *Esquire,* among others, after quitting *The Toronto Daily Star.* The story paints a fierce portrait of two men, a young waiter and an old man, in a Barcelona cafe during the Spanish Civil War. The story is 500-words-short and is excellent magazine writing.

A Clean Well-Lighted Place for Books has recently remodeled and expanded!

A Different Light

489 Castro (at 18th Street)
431-0891
Sun.-Thurs. 10 a.m. - 11 p.m.
Fri.-Sat. 10 a.m. - Midnight

A Different Light carries more than 100 local and national gay- and lesbian-oriented magazines. They handle many gay and lesbian newspapers and newsletters, too.

A Different Light is primarily a bookseller, offering political, philosophical and fiction books. This is a small national chain, with branch stores also located in New York, Hollywood and Los Angeles. Readings and lectures are held regularly at the store.

A-Z Magazines

1392 Ninth Avenue
(btwn. Judah & Irving)
665-4224
Sun.-Thurs. 7 a.m. - 10 p.m.
Fri. 7 a.m. - 11 p.m.
Sat. 8 a.m. - 11 p.m.

This neighborhood magazine stand sells a variety of national magazines and a number of Bay Area newspapers. Because of its central location, it provides nearby UCSF students and neighborhood residents with popular periodicals, smokes and newspapers.

Acorn Books

740 Polk Street
(btwn. Eddy & Ellis)
563-1736
Mon.-Sat. 10:30 a.m. - 8 p.m.
Sun. Noon-7 p.m.

Acorn Books, owned by Joel Chapman, is perhaps San Francisco's most handsome and well-organized used bookstore, offering range, depth and excellent service. Along with Acorn's book selection, one of the City's largest, you might also be interested in the nice collection of *Fortune* magazines that are kept by the sales counter. The store also has an excellent collection of California Historical Society publications and other California history magazines, located in the back room. Hours of enjoyment for all book and magazine lovers.

Austen Books

1687 Haight Street (by Cole)
552-4122
Daily 11 a.m. - 6 p.m.

We include Austen Books for their comprehensive inventory of Dover Publications, the popular clip-art and illustration books. Look for 300 such titles.

Austen Books is a fun, upbeat spot for browsing new and used books. Many pleasant surprises!

Alexander Bookstore

50 Second Street
(btwn. Market & Mission)
495-2992
Mon.-Fri. 8:30 a.m. - 6:30 p.m.
Sat. 10:00 a.m. - 5:00 p.m.

Independently owned and operated by the Stuppin family, Alexander Books is one of SF's largest and most attractive bookstores for new books, with three floors representing well over *60,000* titles. A fine place for books!

Look for a huge fiction section featuring hard-to-find backlists, as well as large sections on philosophy, world studies, history and the arts. While you might find three or four Steinbeck novels in many shops, here you'll find dozens. A well-stocked childrens' book area has proven quite popular, as well, since this downtown bookstore opened just two years ago. (No magazines).

The old-fashioned customer service and special-ordering is noteworthy. With many larger stores watching the bottom line, customer service like this gets rarer everyday. With many book-ordering catalogues and distributor lists available, Alexander Books can help you order that special book, if they haven't got it on the shelf.

A recommended bookstore in the heart of San Francisco's energetic downtown area. Watch for many more new and used bookstores in our next issue...

B. Dalton

Two well-stocked B. Dalton bookstores in San Francisco offer a broad range of domestic and international popular magazines. The downtown store stocks maybe 200 magazine titles.

The stores carry over 25,000 books and periodicals and offer mail-order and phone service. There is also a B. Dalton in Serramonte Center in Daly City (994-1177). Great stores!

200 Kearny
(btwn. Sutter & Bush)
956-2850
Weekdays 9 a.m. - 6 p.m.
Saturdays 10 a.m. - 5 p.m.

Embarcadero Center
982-4278
Weekdays 9:30 a.m. - 6:30 p.m.
Saturdays 10 a.m. - 6 p.m.
Sundays Noon-5 p.m.

Brentano's

Brentano's, a smartly conceived national bookseller, has always been a favorite of magazine browsers. Brentano's stocks over 500 of today's most popular magazines.

The selection of quality books is excellent, with depth, color and range exhibited in the thousands of titles they carry. They also carry an exceptional selection of regional books and local authors, too. Recommended bookstores.

There are three Brentano's in The City:

San Francisco Center
(Fifth & Market)
543-0933
Daily 9:30 a.m. - 8 p.m.

Ghiradelli Square
474-8328
Mon.-Sat. 10 a.m. - 9 p.m.
Sun. 10 a.m. - 6 p.m.

Stonestown Galleria
19th Ave. & Winston Drive
664-6981
Mon.-Sat. 10 a.m. - 9 p.m.
Sun. 11 a.m. - 6 p.m.

The Booksmith
1644 Haight Street
863-8688
Mon.-Sat. 10 a.m. - 9 p.m.
Sun. 10 a.m. - 6 p.m.

The Booksmith is a good bet for magazines, literary journals and popular periodicals. It stocks local news publications and handles a few of the more popular European vogues.

The emphasis at The Booksmith is on a bright, diverse book selection and special-order service. They offer a wide range of materials, attentive buying and a knowledgeable staff. They have a great selection of computer books, health and references, as well as fiction, trade paperbacks and more.

Owned and operated by Gary Frank, Booksmith is one of SF's finest independent bookstores. Open late.

The Book Center
518 Valencia Street (at 16th)
626-2924
Mon.-Sat. 10 a.m. - 6 p.m.

The Book Center features the largest selection of Marxist-Leninist literature in Northern California, selling periodicals on domestic policy issues and movements throughout Asia, Africa and Latin America. (Going through some changes at publication, so do call ahead to check store status).

Builder's Booksource

300 De Haro St. (next to Sally's)
575-3980
Mon.-Sat 9 a.m. - 6 p.m.
Sun. 10 a.m. - 3 p.m.

More and more people are doing their own home addition and remodeling; the thirst for good design and construction books is never fully quenched. Builder's Booksource is The City's best resource for these helpful publications; they carry thousands of titles.

Builder's Booksource has opened a store in San Francisco after their Berkeley store proved to be such a success. The San Francisco store stocks over 4,000 architecture, design and construction resources, books and some magazines. Booksource also sponsors lectures, special events, book-signings and more at their attractive and comfortable South-of-Market bookstore.

They specialize in materials for design professionals in all building fields. They stock City code manuals and have a good selection of woodworking titles. They offer a catalogue and can order many additional titles and software packages. There's a neat kids' section, too.

The original Berkeley store is located at 1817 Fourth Street, (510) 845-6874.

Broadway Cigar and Liquor

550 Broadway (by Columbus)
397-1310

An old WWII tourist guide we looked at listed 18 strip joints in North Beach! Broadway Cigar and Liquor is a monument to those too-bright nights on Broadway during WWII and beyond. It stocks a large selection of magazines and sells mostly soft pornography. By the way, the adjoining Condor Club, infamous for Carol Doda's topless trendsetting, has re-opened as a tourist cafe, featuring coffee drinks and striptease nostalgia.

City Lights Books

261 Columbus Avenue
(by Broadway)
362-8193
Daily 10 a.m. - Midnight

City Lights was the nation's first all-paperback bookstore; it was recently declared a National Literary Landmark by Friends of Libraries USA.

Even though the emphasis is on books, with a large selection of poetry, City Lights' magazine racks are as busy with browsers as any in The City. Owned and operated by Beat poet Lawrence Ferlinghetti and others since 1953, this is a vibrant bookstore that also publishes its own titles. They sometimes close before their "official" closing time of Midnight, call.

China Books & Periodicals

China Books offers an extensive subscription service for periodicals and books from The People's Republic of China. China Books' mail-order catalogue is a local favorite for holiday shopping, offering books on all popular Chinese subjects. There is a wide gift selection covering teas, history, kites and language.

This dynamic collective came of age during the Nixon-in-China years and has become a worldwide conduit for books, periodicals and information from China. They have successfully concentrated their efforts as a mail-order bookseller, while recently re-opening their informal walk-up bookstore at 2931 24th Street. China Books' mailing list is a must for book lovers.

Call China Books to receive their free catalogue by mail at (415) 282-2994 or fax request to 282-0994 (fax).

Cavalli Italian Book Store

1441 Stockton (By Columbus)
421-4219
Mon.-Sat. 9 a.m. - 5:30 p.m.

This North Beach institution has served the Italian community since 1880. Perhaps fifty Italian magazines are displayed and a popular rack vends a dozen local and foreign newspapers. The store also carries books, records and videos from Italy. Cavalli's has an old-world warmth that is rare and becoming rarer in North Beach.

Crown Books

There are three Crown Books stores in San Francisco.

518 Castro Street (by 19th)
552-5213
Sun.-Tues. 10 a.m. - 10 p.m.
Fri., Sat. 10 a.m. - 11 p.m.

740 Clement (btwn. 8th & 9th Avenues)
221-5840
Mon. - Sat. 10 a.m. - 9 p.m.
Sun. 11 a.m. - 5 p.m.

1245 Sutter
(btwn. Polk St. & Van Ness Ave.)
441-7479
Mon.-Sat. 10 a.m. - 9 p.m.
Sun. 11 a.m. - 5 p.m.

Doubleday Book Shop

265 Sutter (btwn. Kearny & Grant)
989-3420
Mon.-Sat. 9:30 a.m. - 6 p.m.
Sun. Noon-5 p.m.

Doubleday carries one of SF's largest selections of domestic and international magazines. There are well over 100 foreign titles and more than 500 American titles. This is a good place to look for many of the more popular magazines and is the only magazine rack in San Francisco with a neon sign!

Drama Books

134 9th Street (by Mission)
255-0604
Mon.-Sat. 10 a.m. - 5 p.m.

De Lauer Super Newsstand

1310 Broadway, Oakland
Open 24 hours daily

Located at the 12th Street Oakland BART entrance, De Lauer sells 12,000 magazines and paperbacks from A-Z. Big on health, science, computers, sports, autos, vogues, populars and everything else.

This may be the largest magazine stand in California, and is certainly the only 24-hour newsstand in town. While you're there, check out photographs of early outdoor De Lauer newsstands, dating back to 1921. Quite a place!

Drama Books carries *Sight & Sound*, *American Film*, *Theatre Crafts*, *Callboard*, *American Theatre*, *Playbill*, *The Drama Review*, *South Atlantic Quarterly*, *The Ross Reports* and more. You may find back issues on occasion. The store has a fine collection of books about the dramatic arts, emphasizing plays, theatre crafts and history. New and used dramatic titles are available.

Eastwind Books

(Chinese-Language)
1435-A Stockton Street
(near Columbus)
781-3331
Mon.-Sat. 10 a.m. - 6 p.m.
Sun. Noon-5 p.m.

(English-Language & Asian Gallery)
633 Vallejo
781-3329

Eastwind Books carries SF's largest and most wide-ranging selection of Chinese, Taiwanese and Hong Kong periodicals, over 500 in all. The stores are owned and operated by a collective; expert help is available for those who are unfamiliar with the materials on hand. The store also carries 10–15,000 book titles ranging from cookbooks to metaphysics. There are large sections dedicated to Eastern arts, and scores of beautifully crafted children's books from Asia. The Vallejo Street shop offers a small gallery of Asian arts.

Goshado Co. Books

1748 Buchanan Street
921-0200
Weekdays 9 a.m. - 6 p.m.
Sat. 10 a.m. - 6 p.m.
Sun. Noon-5 p.m.

This Japantown shop sells a large selection of Japanese books and magazines, records and tapes, gifts and trinkets and Japanese office supplies.

European Book Company

925 Larkin Street
(btwn. Geary & Post)
474-0626
Weekdays 9:30 a.m. - 6 p.m.
Sat. 9:30 a.m. - 5 p.m.

This is a world-class book and magazine importer and distributor, handling English- and foreign-language titles from France, Germany, England, Spain and many other lands. If it's from Europe, they've got it or can get it here.

They have a large selection of magazines, including *Der Spiegel*, *Burda*, *Ratsel*, *Bunte*, *Hola!* and hundreds more. (The German crossword puzzle section is almost overwhelming!)

European Book Company represents San Francisco at her best: inquisitive, international and inspiring. Highly recommended to all.

Eastern News Stand

50 Post (Crocker Galleria)
434-0531
Weekdays 10 a.m. - 6 p.m.
Sat. 10 a.m. - 5 p.m.

This shop is one of a dozen Eastern News Stands supplying bustling business folks with newspapers, magazines and sundry items to make it through the busy work day. This shop offers a well-displayed stock of 250 or more publications.

Forever After Books

1475 Haight Street, by Ashbury
431-8299
Mon.-Sat. 10:30 a.m.-9:30 p.m.
Sun. 11 a.m.-9:30 p.m.

Since 1985, Forever After Books has filled an important niche in SF's rich literary tradition. This respected used-book shop stocks from 30–50,000 titles, specializing in books of timeless, enduring value; history, science fiction, spirituality, health, psychology, true crime, literature and non-fiction.

Obscure books, often ignored by used-booksellers seeking the faster moving titles, are here for readers, researchers and book collectors everywhere. Books are arranged in a creative order that inspires cross-subject title browsing. Reflective new-age sounds lull the book shopper, quality music being a proud tradition of San Francisco bookstores.

Forever After Books carries home and office calendars the year-round, donating remainders to local school teachers for student projects. Cash or trade for used books. Recommended bookstore.

> *We'll soon cover more of SF's used-bookstores such as colorful Haight Street's popular Forever After Books. Literary California offers more bookstores than any state (N.Y. and Texas follow). There's no place for used books like SF and the Bay Area.*

George's News Stand

27 7th Street (off Market)
861-3250
Mon.-Sat. 8 a.m. - Midnight, Sun. 8-6

George's is the true-blue, downtown, magazine and smokeshop. This is one of America's last independent book, magazine and paperback joints. A little much "adult" stock for many, but a monument nonetheless to downtown life and old San Francisco's smokeshop past. Look for the Golden Gate Fields race numbers posted out front...

Good News

3921 24th Street (by Bell Market)
821-3694
Daily until 10 p.m.

Good News is one of San Francisco's newest magazine/newsstands. According to Mr. Richard Seifert, President of L-S Distributors, "A lot of newsstands come and go, opening and closing in a year. Good News just might make it. It's a model SF magazine stand."

Good News offers a great variety and depth in many magazine subjects including style, socio-politics, consumer, hobbies, computers, art, music, sports and vehicles. Look for nearly 1,000 titles in a bright, well-lit shop. Service is exceptional. Next time you come to Noe Valley for an espresso and to shop, drop by Good News, great news for SF magazine browsers.

Harold's

599 Post (corner Post & Taylor)
441-2665
Daily 6 a.m. - 9:30 p.m.

Harold's carries out-of-town newspapers from all over the US and the world and a large stock of American and foreign magazines. If you are looking for *The Jerusalem Post, The New Zealand Herald, The Cork Examiner* or even *The Albuquerque Journal*, Harold's has it. Harold's has a new owner and has just received a shiny new paint job! The premier SF newsstand!

Jack's Smoke Shop

2260 Chestnut Street
(btwn. Scott & Avila)
567-0175
Daily 6 a.m. - 9 p.m.

Jack's is the quintessential cigar and magazine shop. You'll hear great local gossip while you're browsing through hundreds of magazines and newspapers. If you're looking for magazines about sports, the outdoors, fitness or auto racing, try Jack's first. The auto and bike section is one of the largest we've seen. They also carry several score of crossword puzzle books, a lot of "adult" stock and of course, close by the register, your *Player's Forms*!

A very good place for magazines, and a surviving example of the independent smoke-and-magazine days of the past, fading fast. Recommended browsing.

Kinokuniya Bookstores of America

1581 Webster Street (Japan Center)
567-7625
Daily 10:30 a.m. - 7 p.m.

If you're a magazine lover, you will adore Kinokuniya Bookstore in Japantown. The huge San Francisco branch of Japan's largest bookseller will spellbind you. They offer thousands of Japanese- and English-language titles, including entire sections of magazine genres quite different than American standards. The Japanese use colors, textures and techniques that more artistically conservative American publishers might favor in their stationery, but *never* in their magazines!

Titles such as *Whizman*, *Autozam*, *Bears' Club* and *Tarzan* will tantalize you. Arts, sports, interior design, graphics, advertising, fashion, ecology, science, animation: sections of each are large and well-stocked. A real Japanese favorite are the men's and women's comics, with titles such as *Be-Love*, *Me-Twin* and *Lovely-Hi*. If you don't read Japanese, you'll do better in the equally Godzilla-size English-language side of the store. (Prices are marked in yen. Exchange posted.)

The Kiosk
(Three Shops in San Francisco)

If you're pursuing a special title and having no luck, you'll hear it over and over again: "Have you tried The Kiosk?" The problem is, depending on who you ask, The Kiosk seems to be everywhere. We've rounded up the three SF shops for you here. There are several more shops around the Bay Area, but that would just confuse things!

548 Castro (by 19th)
431-3323
Mon.-Thurs. 10 a.m. - 10 p.m.
Fri.-Sat. 10 a.m. - 11 p.m.
Sun. 9 a.m. - 10 p.m.

544 Clement
(btwn. 6th & 7th Avenues)
221-3556
Daily 10 a.m. - 10 p.m.

2050 Chestnut Street
(btwn. Fillmore & Steiner)
474-0569
Daily 10 a.m. - 10 p.m.

The original Haight Street shop has closed. The Kiosk has a new owner, watch for changes.

Last Gasp Comics

2180 Bryant Street
824-6636

Comix distributor Last Gasp carries SF's lion's share of comics and comix, humorous books, blues and jazz titles, cartoons, off-beat videos and more. The *Last Gasp Catalog of Comic Art* is only $1.00 and will open your eyes to a universe of other-world weirdness that's not to be missed.

Raw sex, power, politics, science fiction and standbys such as Zippy the Pinhead make for a fun catalogue just risque enough to receive an R rating. *Weird Smut, The Crab with Golden Claws* and *Tattoo San Francisco* are just a few of thousands of illustrated offerings. If you consider yourself modern and leading edge, you may already have Last Gasp's exotic, erotic and entertaining source book. Call or visit Last Gasp to get yours.

Marcus Bookstore

1712 Fillmore Street (by Post)
346-4222
Mon.-Sat 10 a.m -7 p.m.

Marcus Bookstore opened in 1960, in the early days of the civil rights movement. In thirty years of trying political times, the community store has made active gains. Look for books, literary anthologies, journals and newspapers by, for and about Black people.

The Magazine

731 Larkin
(btwn. Ellis & O'Farrell)
441-7737
Mon.-Sat Noon-7 p.m.

San Francisco's only exclusively used-magazine shop! Owners Trent Dunphy and Robert Mainardi have put together a favorite shop featuring cinema items, much erotica, pulp, pin-ups, military and sports magazines and much more. The transportation section is a special treat. A very deftly selected range of publications and ephemera create an atmosphere for browsing. (They also purchase some old magazines–it's best to call ahead before bringing them by).

Manzanita Books & Records

3686 20th Street
648-0957
Daily Noon-9 p.m.

This is a good place to look for that out-of-print book you need but can't afford to pay $15 for. Poetry, art, music, Native American, esoteric and just plain weird books are featured, as are folk, rock, jazz and classical records. They also have boxes of postcards, old photographs, collectibles and comics of all sorts and there is the San Francisco board game, which you have to see to believe. Don't overlook the popular decorator switchplates. Wayne and David are looking for more stuff to buy or trade for; stop in.

McDonald's Bookshop

48 Turk Street (off Market, near Union Square)
673-2235
Mon., Tues., Thurs. 10 a.m. - 6 p.m.
Wed., Fri., Sat. 10:30 a.m. - 6:45 p.m.

Literally a million magazines, enough to keep you busy for weeks on end! We won't even talk about the one-million or so books, records and more. McDonald's is a SF tradition, legendary for its voluminous stock of used titles and its decrepit, sagging shelves.

A "crazy socialist" named John McDonald started the store some 65 years ago, and once it began growing, well...seeing is believing.

Modern Times

888 Valencia
282-9246
Weekdays 11 a.m. - 8 p.m.
Sat. 11 a.m. - 6:30 p.m.
Sun. 11 a.m. - 5 p.m.

Modern Times offers a good-sized set of magazine racks featuring publications with an emphasis on Central American, South American, Chinese and Third World issues. The shop is operated by a collective and carries one of SF's best collections of children's books and a range of materials on feminism, gay rights and progressive movements around the world.

Museum Books

SF Museum of Modern Art
401 Van Ness Avenue
252-4035
Tues., Wed., Fri. 10 a.m. - 6 p.m.
Thurs. 11 a.m. - 9 p.m.
Sat.-Sun. 11 a.m. - 5:30 p.m.

Although they don't carry very many magazines, Museum Books does stock the lion's share of art, design and graphics books. Many beautiful children's books, stationery and gifts, but the emphasis is definitely on books, design and art. Recommended browsing.

The Naked Eye

533 Haight Street
(btwn. Fillmore & Steiner)
864-2985
Weekdays 10 a.m. - 10 p.m.
Sat. 10 a.m. - 11 p.m.
Sun. 11 a.m. - 10 p.m.

Naked Eye carries the stuff you'll never find at Brentano's. Titles such as *Film Threat, Primal Chaos, The Skeptical Enquirer, Murder Can Be Fun* (an annual calendar of collected murder highlights), *Bad Attitudes* (S&M meets art) and many of the more popular 'zines, both local and national, are here. They also carry an extensive and way far-out video selection. A popular late-night haunt in the Lower Haight.

Ninth Avenue Books

1348 9th Avenue
(btwn. Irving & Judah)
665-2938
Mon.-Thurs. 10 a.m. - 9 p.m.
Fri.-Sun. 10 a.m. - 10 p.m.

Ninth Avenue Books is a bright, friendly bookstore, popular with Sunset shoppers and nearby UCSF faculty and students. There is a nice set of magazine racks near the door. The shop handles special orders, will help you with title searches and offers gift wrapping.

Ninth Avenue Books is the sister store to The Richmond's popular Green Apple Books. Both are recommended for their large inventories, rich scope and truly independent status. They have the finest managers, buyers and staff to serve you.

Small Press Traffic

3599 24th Street (at Guerrero)
285-8394
Tues.-Sat. Noon - 6 p.m.

This non-profit bookstore and writers' center offers many literary periodicals, often available only by subscription or mail order. Poetry, art and fiction are the main thrust, with thousands of unique small press titles. A great place to browse for poetry and fiction books. Recommended.

Old Wives' Tales

1009 Valencia (at 21st Street)
821-4676
Weekdays (except Thurs.) 11 a.m. - 7 p.m.
Thurs. 11 a.m. - 9 p.m.
Sat.-Sun. 11 a.m. - 6 p.m.

Owned and operated by The Old Wives' Tales Collective, this large bookstore offers a good selection of periodicals dedicated to feminism and women's issues. It came of age during the '80s, a period of widespread indifference to these concerns. They handle 12,000 books and periodicals through the store's complete ordering service. A catalogue is available. They fill mail orders all over the world and will help you with subscriptions to feminist and lesbian newsletters and periodicals.

San Francisco Scout Shop

186 2nd Street (near Market)
543-2552
Weekdays 8:30 a.m. - 5 p.m.
Sat. 9 a.m. - 3 p.m.

If you don't have a copy of *The Boy Scout Handbook*, you're missing out. This full-color 600-page master-book holds a world full of camping, cooking, knot-tying and other useful lessons that come in handy time after time, even in our urban life. The Scout motto, after all, is *Be Prepared*. Merit badge books range from *Archery* to *Veterinary Science*. The Scout Shop has a full range of popular nature books. *Golden Guides*, too, and *Boys' Life*.

Pacific Heights Pharmacy

2436 Fillmore
346-0707
Weekdays 10 a.m. - 6:30 p.m.
Sat. 10 a.m. - 5 p.m.

Pacific Heights has changed a great deal over the past several decades, particularly along Fillmore Street, known to many simply as "The Fillmore."

There are little moments of history in Pacific Heights, and one is this pharmacy, drug store and newsstand, founded in the 1920s by Tom Merigan (now owned by Gene Nagase).

Before the advent of giant drugstore chains such as Walgreen Drugs and Merrill's, independent pharmacies like this one played a major role in the distribution of magazines during the renaissance of the American magazine in the 1920s.

Pacific Heights Pharmacy carries a very large selection of popular magazines and paperbacks, cards, gifts and, of course, prescriptions. It is a handsome example of the American pharmacy. (Several local pharmacies have closed these past two years, including Richard Barberian's Overland Drug and Jack Vaupen's Vaupen Drugstore.)

By offering neighborhood service, Pacific Heights Pharmacy still survives the changes of "progress."

SF Cameraworks

70 12th Street
(by Mission/South Van Ness)
621-1001
Tues.-Sun. Noon-5 p.m.

SF Cameraworks is a non-profit gallery, resource group and bookstore for local photographers and photo/multimedia artists. This energetic group offers a range of photo "ops" for film artists and professionals.

We hope to spend a little more time with them next year, but for now we would like to recommend their bookstore to those searching for local and regional books, magazines and newsletters dedicated to photography.

Art/photo periodicals such as *ReSearch, Cinematograph, Parachute* and *ArtPaper* are available here, as well as many art/photo books created and published by SF's own photographers. The excellent *SF Cameraworks Quarterly*, their own periodical, is one of more than 100 titles available here.

Located at the top floor of an old warehouse, SF Cameraworks holds a continuing gallery series, too. SF Cameraworks is a non-profit resource supported by memberships and private and public sponsors, including Eastman Kodak.

49

**Half Dome
Yosemite Valley**

Sierra Club Store
730 Polk Street (by Eddy)
923-5600
Weekdays 10 a.m. - 5:30 p.m.
Saturdays 10 a.m. - 5 p.m.

The Sierra Club was founded a century ago by John Muir. Muir, who came to California from Scotland at age 11, spent most of his life studying the mountains, valleys, glaciers and wildlife of California and Alaska. One of the foremost advocates of our National Parks, he publicized the region's natural beauties in his popular books, sold worldwide.

Today, the Sierra Club Store continues that tradition, offering outstanding books about nature and the outdoors, with a regional bent. There's a lot of California out there...

Tower Books and Magazines

Tower Books and Magazines has three Bay Area locations, each of which is open from 9 a.m. to Midnight, 365 days a year.

Concord
1280 E. Willow Pass Rd.,
(510) 827-2920

San Mateo
2727 El Camino Real, (415) 570-7444

Mountain View
630 San Antonio Rd., (415) 941-7300

Look for many magazine titles here that you won't find anywhere else! Tower Books and Magazine hunts for these titles in order to stock a diverse range of books, music and magazines.

Tower began with a small section of be-bop and blues records in a Sacramento pharmacy years ago. Today, Tower has book, video and music store locations throughout the world. The North Beach Tower Records at Columbus Ave. & Bay Street (885-0500) is the chain's excellent flagship store in The City.

(Also, watch for the ALMANAC, coming soon to Tower stores in the Bay Area, Manhattan and even Japan! Thanks to Tower's Doug Biggert and crew for the energetic attention to regional and local publications and magazines.)

U.S. Government Bookstore

The Federal Building (off lobby)
450 Golden Gate Ave.
(btwn. Polk & Larkin)
556-6657
Weekdays 8 a.m. - 3:30 p.m.

One of 23 Government Printing Office retail outlets in the United States, this store is a "catalogue-order" showroom; only a small portion of all US government periodicals, maps, charts, posters and books are in stock.

Pick up the brochure *Government Periodicals and Subscription Services* at the door. They stock periodic background notes on hundreds of countries, the 500 or so journals that make up the Code of Federal Regulations, government directories, trademark and copyright materials and hundreds of home improvement and trade books. Trust us! If you're a mail order junkie, this place will keep your mailbox buzzing!

Znanie Book Store

5237 Geary Blvd. (by 16th Avenue)
752-7555
Mon.-Sat. 10 a.m. - 6 p.m.

If you want to know more about Mother Russia, Znanie's subscription catalogue includes 300 newspapers and 2,000 magazines. *Agrikultura Moldovei, Kommunist, Slovesnik* and *Volga* are a few of the titles available; the service also includes literary, medical, science, sports and kids' categories.

Waldenbooks

Waldenbooks, quality discount sister-store to Brentano's, carries several hundred magazine titles and many thousands of popular books on all subjects. They are neighborhood bookstores, popular for their rich selections and discount prices. You'll find two stores in The City and a store in Serramonte. Call for convenient hours.

2169 Chestnut
(btwn. Steiner & Pierce)
563-1658

255 West Portal Avenue
(btwn. 14th & Vicente)
664-7596

122 Serramonte Center
Daly City (off I-280)
755-3373

The History of A Magazine King

Richard Seifert and L-S Distributors

Nobody knows magazines (and books) like Dick Seifert, President of L-S Distributors. He's been San Francisco's premier book and magazine source these past forty years.

In a two-hour whirlwind tour of his career and the industry he has led, we got a glimpse of his remarkable career. The story of his efforts could span the length of a movie— a tale of innovation and marketing courage, with a little bit of luck as well. Dick's efforts have paid off and success has come his way at every turn. In this cut-throat cigar-box and pennies business, that's remarkable. What's more, he's the nicest guy you'll ever meet...

In 1952, 22-year-old Dick Seifert reported for his first day of work at Golden Gate News Agency, 66 3rd Street at Mission. He liked what he saw. The neighborhood was, to say the least, colorful. Upon entering the shop he saw expensive foreign cigarettes, fancy imported candies, the best German peppermints—a real paradise.

Dick set to work at his appointed task, bookkeeping. He was placed in charge of, among many financial tasks, the distribution of the Sunday *New York Times*, delivered by train each Thursday. On a good week he'd handle as many as twenty orders of the thick Eastern paper, mostly to the Fairmont, the Mark Hopkins, the St. Francis and other City hotels. This was young Seifert's introduction to the distribution business.

When Dick came to Golden Gate News Agency there were approximately 1,000 so-called ID's (independent distributors) in the US. They distributed leading national magazines, including *Time, Newsweek* and *Look*. They were exclusive agents for the big publishers.

Golden Gate began to look for new products and new ways to bring these items to retailers. One way they did this was by offering titles that the ID's wouldn't or couldn't offer. In an era of lingering Victorian attitudes and fast-changing sexual values, PG-rated erotica was a natural departure. Although Golden Gate did not handle any pornography, *One, Inc.*, a leading gay men's magazine, and a similiar title offered by the Daughters of Bilitis, a prominent lesbian group, sold well. Another popular line was the "Swedish nudist magazine," airbrushed girlie mags thinly disguised as "figure studies." Although all are tame by today's standards, they were ignored by the ID's and Dick and his group picked up a profitable market.

The business grew as Golden Gate became the only source for "alternative" titles in the conservative postwar years. They were the first local distributor for *The National Enquirer*, then considered too risque by the ID's.

In the 1950s paperbacks became popular, forever changing the book world. *Pocket Books, Cardinal Giants* and others sold for a dime, a quarter, then fifty cents. There was limited competition because short-sighted booksellers felt paperbacks were low-end and tacky. Dick found that pharmacies, corner stores and hotel shops didn't share this view, and they sold plenty of copies.

From a single station-wagon, the growing company, now called L-S Distributors (L-S stands for Louis Swift, Dick's Golden Gate News mentor) vended the popular new product. Eventually Dick expanded their service with a small fleet of new ($2,200.00) VW delivery vans.

One day a young magazine editor named Hugh Hefner came through the door, asking Seifert if L-S Distributors would carry his soon-to-be published title *Playboy,* banned outright by the ID's. L-S was exclusive agent of *Playboy*, until the powerful ID's warmed up to the cash earnings and took over distribution. (This was not an uncommon occurrence. Dick's group often broke a lot of ground, only to lose a title to the ID's after their early commitment proved its sale potential).

By the mid-1960s, L-S had become old hands at the paperback game. America was opening up to brave new ideas, and small-publisher "trade paperbacks" and small magazines brought that culture to readers. L-S had already established itself as a pioneer in this market and was poised for the explosion of "grass roots" publications. Trade paperbacks such as *Our Bodies, Ourselves* and *The Whole Earth Catalog* turned to L-S for distribution. A rash of small magazines with big ideas appeared out of the confusion. Jann Wenner walked into L-S and pitched his *Rolling Stone Magazine* to Dick and his crew. *The Psychedelic Review,* published by a Haight-Ashbury group, was a big hit, too. *Creem Magazine* also joined the L-S title list. By 1970, L-S Distributors had arrived.

Today, L-S Distributors continues to support those publications too small to go national, stocking many book titles you'll never find on the best-seller lists. They have come from an independent background and continue to support independent publishers.

Book selling for the small publisher remains a difficult task at best. A book's sales depends on the readers available and the publisher's ability to bring those readers in. For those who offer a serious product and get fully behind it, L-S will always do its best to bring that title to the buyers, who'll then purchase a book or magazine depending on demand. When a title does well, the people at L-S are as pleased as anyone.

Today, L-S Distributors runs a brisk delivery and cash-and-carry warehouse operation, offering retailers the opportunity to purchase over 20,000 book and magazine titles at discount prices for resale. Many specialty shops have realized that books offer a profitable addition to their retail line, add color and richness to their store and bring new shoppers into the fold.

We asked Dick about the future of books and magazines in the computer and CD age.

"CD-ROM is coming fast. It's like the VCR's, you know. When everyone has an optical CD device (computer), much of it will go that way. Digital items are available now, particularly dictionaries and directories. It makes sense already, it's available and they're using it. Besides, the CD revolution will offer the small publisher a fresh new horizon. They'll be able to reach their readers without the large expenses of paper, printing and binding. When it happens, we're ready and able."

Our interview drew to an end. The good magazine king paused, then closed in a royal booklover's fashion.

"People will always buy books and magazines. The feel of a book—the smell of the paper and ink. People and their books and magazines have been together forever, through thick and thin. My bet—they're here to stay."

Call L-S Distributors at 873-2094 or 1-800-654-7040 for information on their book and magazine distribution service. Their warehouse, located at 130 East Grand Avenue just off of Highway 101, is open Monday through Saturday from 8 a.m. until 5 p.m.

Books, Paper & Ink

CITY LIGHTS Bookseller

POCKET · BOOK · SHOP ·

City Lights Bookseller & Publisher, since 1953

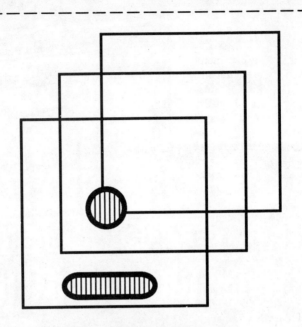
Computer user-groups provide IBM or Macintosh users with opportunities to meet other folks working with computers, see new software and hardware demonstrated and take home low-cost "shareware." Meetings are held on a regular basis. Bring blank diskettes to meetings. Call Berkeley Macintosh Users Group (BMUG) at (510) 759-4604 or USF/Golden Gate Mac Users Group at (415) 666-2978. We'll bring you more...

Feng Shui

Feng Shui, pronounced "foong suey," is the series of principles by which the Chinese determine the placement of exterior entrances and landscapes of buildings. Translated, *Feng* means wind and *Shui* means water. The codism was first scribed in the 9th Century AD by a famous scholar named Yang Yunsung. Practitioners of *Feng Shui* are called geomancers and use a tool called a *Lo Pan,* which is a predecessor of the compass. Long before the earth's magnetism was understood, geomancers felt two kinds of energy: *chi,* a beneficial form of energy that meandered gently along irregular paths, and *sha,* an ill-starred form of energy that travels in straight lines with evil impact. Read Shirley Fong-Torres' *Chinatown: A Walking Tour* for a complete explanation of this still highly-respected practice in Chinese architecture.

Chinatown:

A Walking Tour with Shirley Fong-Torres

Shirley Fong-Torres has an ideal perspective to write a guide to this fascinating San Francisco neighborhood. She is the daughter of a Chinese restaurant family and now works as a tour organizer. This book is a local jewel and we suggest you buy it for your next visit to Chinatown.

The rich little paperback features history, shopping with the locals, medicine business, tea, brush painting and lots and lots of good Chinese recipes. Fresh, informative guide to Chinese life and Chinatown. Call China Books & Periodicals to order it at 282-2994, weekdays 9 a.m. - 5 p.m., or ask at your local bookstore. Just $10.95.

See "Wok Wiz" tour of Chinatown in the Fun Day Trips *section of this* ALMANAC. *Here's a recipe for Chinese garlic spinach from Shirley's must-have book:*

Chinese Garlic Spinach From *Chinatown: A Walking Tour*

2 bunches
fresh spinach
1 T. vegetable oil
4 or 5 cloves
minced garlic
¼ cup chicken
broth

Clean spinach, trim roots and cut leaves and stems into two-inch pieces. Drain and dry. Heat wok with oil. When smoky, stir-fry garlic until golden brown. Immediately add spinach and cook over high heat for two minutes. Stir in chicken broth and continue to cook until spinach becomes wilted but is still green and the broth evaporates. Serve immediately.

MANZANITA BOOKS 3686 20th St.

ADOBE BOOKS 3166 16th St.

ROUND≈WORLD MUSIC 491a Guerrero St.

LA PAJARITA 3125 16th St.

VALENCIA BOOKS 524 Valencia St.

CAFE BEANO/THE MARSH 878 Valencia St.

A BOOK-LOVER'S GUIDE TO THE MISSION

A Book Lover's Guide to the Mission

This pocket-sized map of the bookstores and cafes of the Mission District is available at Manzanita Used Books and Records, 3686 20th Street at Guerrero, 648-0957 (see *Magazine & Booksellers of SF*). Elizabeth Newman contributed the artwork and Wayne Holder edited this unique little (free) map. Look for more Book Lover's Guides to other neighborhoods in the future!

Book Finder

Compiled and published by Jules Greenblatt of Mountain View, California, the *Northern California Book Finder*, now in its sixth edition, lists hundreds of the used-bookstores in the Bay Area and carries helpful display ads from many. If you are looking for a specific book title from the past, this "let-your-fingers-do-the-walking" pocket-size used-bookstore reference will serve you well. To give you an idea, we picture the book above, and a sample ad from Albatross Books, one of San Francisco's best used-book haunts. Send $7.50 to Jules Greenblatt, 1050 Crestview Drive #5, Mountain View CA, 94040; (415) 968-2341.

A FOOL'S WAY

I stumble through life,
fighting with shadows
who pull me to dark floors;
money flies through my hands
like water away from a net;
hunger fills the night—
yet the book of Chinese poetry which
perfects this night cost only $1.35!
Reading it, I find the
Great Dragon Universe is my room!
So great a fool I am, I hear the farthest
stars laughing.
"When will you wake up?"
they wonder with a mother's love—

—Paul Meyers

Compliments of the Haight Ashbury
Literary Journal, *available at The
Booksmith, City Lights and Bound
Together Bookstores; costs only $1.50!*

The Sunset Beacon

San Franciscans looking for local news
are often frustrated by the difficulty of
finding it. *The Sunset Beacon* is a great
source for City news, a publication
that puts news on par with advertising
and digs for local stories. It is a sister
publication to *The Richmond Review*.

The Sunset Beacon features in-depth
coverage of neighborhood day-to-day
reality, focusing on small business and
City Hall activity that affects its readers most strongly, with a particular
emphasis on the huge Sunset District.
Crime reports, community events, local history, public meetings and great
people features have made this fine
newspaper a popular success. Advertising in this newspaper gets results,
according to numerous businesses we
have spoken to, which is a testimony to
its faithful readership.

Newsracks are located at Safeway at
17th Ave. and Taraval, Walgreen Drugs
at 22nd and Taraval, Sunset Super at
2425 Irving Street and UCSF's Milberry Union, among several dozen
places. Edited and published by Chris
Rivers and Paul Kozakiewicz. Call 664-
0415 with editorial or advertising inquiries. Monthly, free-circulated.

Each year THE ALMANAC *highlights a
favorite local newspaper. We thank
these local editors for their attention to
the community in The City.*

Book Passage

Book Passage, a complete traveler's bookstore, is located at 51 Tamal Vista Blvd. in Corte Madera. Book Passage's rich catalogue features several thousand travel books, magazines and tape selections that are available by mail.

In Search of Your British and Irish Roots, written by Angus Baxter, helps you trace your English, Welsh, Scottish or Irish ancestors. The book lists surname organizations, county record offices in Europe, marriage and will bureaus and more (#11485—$19.95). *'Round Ireland in Low Gear* is a witty recap of a bicycle tour of the Emerald Isle taken by author Eric Newby and his wife. This simple Irish venture became...well, call it the luck of the Irish (#11339—$8.95). Call the Book Passage to order their free catalogue at (415) 927-0960 or 1-800-321-9785.

Star Rover House

Lexikos Press, a local publisher that publishes local books, offers *Star Rover House,* an imprint that has reprinted 51 of Jack London's novels. The charming and quite inexpensive reprints will make for months of seat-of-the-pants reading as the Bay Area's own Jack London tells tales of Yukon trappers, Indian lore and maritime exploration and suspense. Many of the novels, including *Tales of the Fish Patrol*, chronicle London's boyhood sailing adventures on San Francisco Bay. Lexikos' catalogue is one of the most compelling we've seen, a little booklet packed with good suggested reads.

Other fine Lexikos titles include *Shipwrecks at the Golden Gate* by James Delgado and Stephen Haller, accomplished local historians, and *Boss Gardener: The Life and Times of John McLaren,* by Tom Aikman. This biography paints a personal portrait of the man who ran Golden Gate Park for nearly fifty years and developed much of the Park as we know it today. *The Making of Golden Gate Park, The Growing Years 1906-1950*, written by the late Raymond Clary, is a must for anyone wanting to understand the colorful history of Golden Gate Park.

Call Lexikos at 488-0401 to order this catalogue, a treasure chest of books.

pine & oak
finished & unfinished
custom & standard

BOOKSHELVES

759-1234
515 Frederick Street
(at Stanyan)
San Francisco, CA 94117

The Family Travel Guides Catalogue

Call Carousel Press Editor and Publisher Carole Meyers to order this delightful mail-order book and periodical catalogue that offers travel opportunities for families and kids. Carousel Press also offers an assortment of travel papers and informal and very current newsletters spotlighting popular vacation and travel locations in the US and around the world. Call (510) 527-5849.

NOE VALLEY
3910 Twenty-fourth Street
near Sanchez
San Francisco, 94114
(415) 282-8080

Cover-to-Cover Kids

Cover to Cover Booksellers at 3910 24th Street in Noe Valley, 282-8080, is well-established as one of the Bay Area's finest bookstores for children's books. Next ALMANAC issue we plan to fully cover the extensive SF new and used-bookstore world, and we plan to review many local favorites such as cozy, energetic Cover-to-Cover.

Heyday Books
News from Native California

Heyday Books' catalogue is a must-have for those with an interest in this Bay Area we love to call home. Their selection of local books by talented local writers includes subjects such as the Native American life, natural history, Alcatraz, California writers Jack London and John Steinbeck, regional parks, parking in San Francisco and bicycling in the Bay Area. These affordable, quality paperbacks have sharp, clean design.

News from Native California is a unique and entertaining quarterly magazine that provides an inside view of Native American history and culture, written and produced by California Indians and those close to their community. Each issue has lively columns and articles on art, ongoing and upcoming events, language, recipes, traditional skills, political concerns and more.

Beautifully designed and printed, and illustrated with dozens of historical and modern photographs, *News from Native California* is not only a source of up-to-date Native American news, but also an important historical archive. Subscriptions are $16.00 a year for four issues.

Call Heyday Books in Berkeley at 1-800-536-3564 to receive their free catalogue or to order the above title.

HEYDAY BOOKS

All the Tea in China...

Known throughout Asia as one of China's great treasures, tea is second only to water as a world beverage. Tea has been linked with health from the very beginning. It is prized for its ability to banish fatigue, stimulate mental powers and raise the energy level.

The Taoist philosophers and Buddhist monks, who did much to improve tea and encourage its cultivation in China, invested tea with greater meaning than any other beverage.

All the Tea in China is a comprehensive and fun book covering the entire range of tea lore. Authors Kit Chow and Ione Kramer are renowned China/tea experts from East and West.

The book includes thousands of fun and enriching tea items from throughout history and around the world, including tea traditions and history; customs, rites and ceremonies; Japanese art of tea; ceramics and tea "equipage"; tea and health and 50 famous Chinese teas.

It is a remarkably complete book, entertaining, educational and enlightening—a great resource!

Available at China Books and Periodicals, *All The Tea in China* is just $14.95 and is available by easy mail order with check, MasterCard or Visa. Call China Books at 282-2994 to order. One of many fine China Books titles. (See China Books listing in *Magazine and Booksellers of SF*.)

Maps

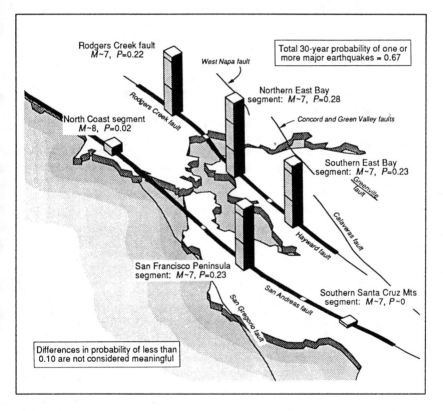

Rodgers Creek fault
$M \sim 7$, $P=0.22$

West Napa fault

Total 30-year probability of one or more major earthquakes = 0.67

Northern East Bay segment: $M \sim 7$, $P=0.28$

Concord and Green Valley faults

Rodgers Creek fault

North Coast segment $M \sim 8$, $P=0.02$

Southern East Bay segment: $M \sim 7$, $P=0.23$

Greenville fault

Calaveras fault

Hayward fault

San Francisco Peninsula segment: $M \sim 7$, $P=0.23$

Southern Santa Cruz Mts segment: $M \sim 7$, $P \sim 0$

San Andreas fault

San Gregorio fault

Differences in probability of less than 0.10 are not considered meaningful

30-YEAR PROBABILITIES (P) OF LARGE EARTHQUAKES (M ≥7) IN THE SF BAY REGION

COLUMN HEIGHTS ARE PROPORTIONAL TO 30-YEAR PROBABILITY OF EARTHQUAKE
UNITED STATES GEOLOGICAL SURVEY/NEPEC 1988–1991 WORKING GROUP REPORT

San Francisco Maps & Map Sellers

San Francisco: City of Maps

From current BART/Muni travel maps and the popular "criss-cross" directories to scenic mural and aerial maps in offices and museums throughout San Francisco, this city has maps!

We've included many maps and map-sellers here and some of the good old maps we've purchased in our pursuit of San Francisco's oh-so-present past. Read *Little Libraries* for more sources and be sure to visit the map index catalog at the San Francisco History Room at the Main Library.

Thomas Brothers Maps & Books at 550 Jackson Street (981-7520) sells an extensive array of international and local maps, books, globes and guides, including the entire line of Thomas Brothers' "Popular Street Atlases." Thomas Bros. has been a leader in the map industry since its founding here in San Francisco back in 1915. Call 1-800-899-6277 for other Thomas Bros. map dealers around the Bay. Validated parking available at the lot at Jackson and Sansome Streets. A great resource for contemporary maps of The City and the surrounding Bay Area.

The Rand McNally Map and Travel Store at 595 Market Street (at 2nd) sells the entire spectrum of NY-based Rand McNally's maps, travel guides, atlases and the north-south-east-west rest. Each Christmas they publish a Holiday catalog for mail-orders. Drop by the pleasant store to shop or browse next time you're in the Financial District. Open weekdays 9 a.m. - 6 p.m. and Saturdays 10 a.m. - 4 p.m.

The Map Center, 2440 Bancroft Way in Berkeley, (510) 841-6277, sells US Forest Service maps, USGS maps, trail maps for The Sierras and other California parks and trails, nautical charts for The Bay and surrounding waters and much more. They sell a wide range of the popular Sierra Club Wilderness Press topographic maps, too. They have no catalog, but do offer mail-order when necessary. Just call and ask and the friendly staff will help you find what you want. The Map Center has another store in Santa Clara, too, call (408) 296-6277.

If you know of other unique maps, please write or call so that we may include them in future issues. Call or write THE ALMANAC at: 1657 Waller Street #A, SF, CA 94117 or 1-800-352-5268. Share your "Native Wisdom" with your fellow readers!

The USGS Library/Bookstore at 555 Battery, The Custom House, 5th floor, sells an extensive selection of maps for hiking and trails and USGS special survey maps for the Bay Area. This is a particularly good place to search for information about soils and seismology, offering mapped soils surveys of San Francisco and the Bay Area as well as earthquake intensity surveys, earthquake probability reports, land use maps, flood plain surveys and more.

Almost everything sold is published by the United States Geological Survey, The US Department of Interior or the US Government Printing Office; you'll be impressed with how far your subsidized map-buying dollar will stretch. The bookstore staff is highly trained in geology and maps and they are able to answer many of the specific or technical questions you might have. Open weekdays 9 a.m. - 4 p.m.; call 705-1010 for information. Here are some particularly relevant USGS titles, all about $5.00:

Probabilities of Large Earthquakes in the San Francisco Bay Region, CA (USGS Circular 1053)

Geologic Principles for Prudent Land Use—A Decision-Maker's Guide for The San Francisco Bay Region (Paper 946)

Flood-Prone Area and Land-Use Planning, Selected Examples from the San Francisco Bay Region (Paper 942)

The Map Room at City Hall, Room 352, is, to say the least, intriguing. Here the plat maps of City surveys are kept. In 1906 all of the maps of The City were supposedly destroyed in the third day of the great fire. In the ensuing aftermath, almost the entire City was re-surveyed for boundaries and over the years the plats have been transferred to huge sheets of clear plastic. Changes to survey plats are drawn on these large erasable maps as they occur. Frankly, this Editor has trouble with the concept of recording the entire key-map of The City onto one of the most flammable substances around, but alas, it's City Hall.

The late historian Raymond Clary revealed to us that he believed that the supposedly burned pre-1906 maps are possibly stored with a massive body of other City archives at a local storage facility and were **not** burned in the Great Fire. His research relates that City Hall did not burn until the third day of the great 1906 conflagration and that men and horsecarts dragged a huge percentage of the valuable City documents to a warehouse on "The Miracle Mile," as Mission Street was called in those days, and later to where it sits today, while The City pays the long-term storage costs.

Perhaps an interested group of go-get-'em historians would look into this? This may be the mother-lode of pre-quake documents everybody wants!

The San Francisco History Room at the Main Library, 3rd Floor, 557-4567, has compiled the entire contents of the famous *R.L. Polk and Co. City Directories (Criss-Cross Maps)* onto convenient, easily printable microfilm. The maps date from the 19th Century and were updated annually through the years. They indicate the names of the owners of lots and parcels, businesses located at each address and land use in The City. They offer access by address and phone number (for later maps) and by name of owner or business. Located in the Newspaper Room. Please do ask for help with microfilm if you are new to it. The staff will be glad to help you get started.

A San Francisco History Room volunteer spearheaded the complex microfilm indexing task for another set of important maps, *The Sanborn Insurance Maps,* poring over pieces and scraps of the aging maps for the past few years. They are located in the Newspaper Room, too. It takes a little time to get adjusted to the maps and viewing procedures, since the maps are square and microfilm isn't, but you get the hang of it after awhile. (A research study we recently did at THE ALMANAC centered on a lot and parcel that for some reason seemed to fall just off the edge of every map we indexed! We really learned to appreciate the difficult task of indexing these maps for microfilm.)

Maps Around The City

Here are maps and resources that contribute further to the "big picture" of SF's growth and change since 1849.

Photographic Mural Map of Bay Front, Russian Hill, North Beach and Nob Hill, 1865—North Beach Museum, upper lobby Eureka Savings Bank, 1435 Stockton Street at Columbus. Open bank hours. (Map is located on the wall as you descend from the upper-lobby level.)

Special Soils Areas Maps
Room 203, Bureau of Building Inspection (BBI), 450 McAllister Street. *SSA Maps* for sale indicate "Special Soil Areas" (SSA's) deemed unstable by BBI's Plans Approval Division and The Board of Supervisors under the post-1989 earthquake/building repair-code legislation for wood-frame dwellings (Victorians) as provided by Bill 103-90. SSA mapping is an ongoing process, according to map-keeper Pervez Patel of BBI. Maps are about $6.00 and were drawn from USGS studies and others.

> "History never looks like history when you're living through it. It looks confusing and messy and it always feels uncomfortable."
>
> —John Gardner

Aerial Map of San Francisco, 1950s

Pacific Security Bank, 2400 Noriega Street, in Lobby. This huge aerial photo map measures 25 ft. by 12 ft.!

Seismic Impact Maps of The City

The Museum of the City and County of San Francisco, The Cannery, 2501 Leavenworth St. Displayed is a *Guide Map of San Francisco* from 1907 that clearly shows the utter destruction that the 1906 earthquake unleashed. Call 928-0289.

The Burnham Plan for San Francisco, 1905

This map series is available in a book at The San Francisco History Room. Burnham was hired by The City to redesign San Francisco and took hundreds of photographs of The City from Twin Peaks, where he kept a studio, and from other bird's-eye locations about town. The great earthquake and fire brought many of his designs into use, incorporated in the complete reconstruction of SF after the 1906 quake and fire.

Map of San Francisco, 1887

The Boxing Museum, 3rd Floor Hallway, Civic Auditorium (99 Grove). This is a nice map of San Francisco as it expanded toward the ocean. There are other old maps and photos of The City here, too. Boxing fans should drop by soon. (See Boxing Museum review in *Little Libraries and Museums*).

Block & Parcel Map

At the entrance to The City Assessor's Office, Room 106 at City Hall, you'll find a 1982 map of every surveyed lot in San Francisco and its lot number.

Cartoon Map of SF, 1927

A reader, Eric Zo, told us about this delightful repro-map of San Francisco available at Forever After Books, 1475 Haight Street by Ashbury (431-8299) and at Green Apple Books, near the stairs to the second level.

The colored patina map features every recognizable landmark of the era in the style of local cartoonists (drawn by Harrison Godwin). It features cartoon histories, army tents at The Presidio, banks, stage and screen-house drawings, post-quake humor notes, cartoon pioneers, bathing beauties, school-lot bullies and more. Fun map!

Map Hunt On—

If anyone knows where THE ALMANAC Editor can get ahold of a copy of a map called (this is a long one): *Map of the Outside Lands of the City and County of San Francisco Showing Reservations for Public Purposes under the Provision of Order No. 800 as Surveyed by Monroe Ashbury in 1868,* please call or write The Editor. The map is one of the earliest accurate maps of the lands that became The Haight, The Richmond and The Sunset, as The City expanded west to the Pacific.

Relief Map of the Bay Area Showing Quakes +3M, from 1808-1989

This neat map is one of several, along with a working seismograph, at The Randall Museum. This is one of the best earthquake exhibits in The City (see *Little Libraries & Museums.*)

Harris Real Estate Map, GG Park

Done in 1892 to promote the sale of lots in the expanding Richmond and Sunset Districts, this pictorial map at the information desk at the Russell Library at Strybing Arboretum is neat! (See *Little Libraries & Museums.*)

Redwood Ring—Growth Timeline

A slice of old-growth redwood, 1550–1935, helps us put modern Bay Area history in perspective. The long gaps of notation prior to the 18th Century indicate an admitted lack of understanding of Bay Area Native American history. Located at The Randall Museum. (See *Little Libraries and Museums.*)

1872 Map of Yerba Buena

This is one of the finest maps of early San Francisco available to historians. There is a fine example at Treasure Island Museum, as you enter exhibits.

San Francisco Map Binders

The San Francisco History Room at the Main Library has photocopies of many of its maps, kept in easily accessible notebooks for index and reference. Hundreds of maps of The City are available for quick reference.

Map Room
The Doe Library,
UC-Berkeley

Room 137, near the bell tower
(510) 642-4940
Weekdays 10 a.m. - 5 p.m.
Saturdays 1 p.m. - 5 p.m.
(closed summer and recess)

For those with a love or interest in maps, this room will forever enrich your life. Approximately 50 six-foot-tall flat files store maps from every country, period and purpose; copies are available while-you-wait. We found the collection of pre-1906 San Francisco maps a bit thin, with perhaps a few more on hand at the SF Public Library's San Francisco Room, but if you are searching for SF maps, there's plenty to warrant the trip to Berkeley.

Highlights are a 1906 map done in late April following the quake and a very large and quite stunning framed map measuring 8 ft. by 5 ft. showing the developed portions of SF in 1854. The room is comfortable, map access is easy and the range of US and international maps is unparalleled in California. Look for 300,000 maps, over 5,000 atlases and references and 52,000 aerial photos of Northern California, all compiled on the GLADIS computer system for ease of access. Look for the collection of satellite pictures. Light tables, measuring devices and other map aids are available. Non-UCB patrons welcome. The staff is quite helpful.

More Maps

CA Division of Mines and Geology
380 Civic Drive, Suite 100
Pleasant Hill, CA (510) 646-5920
Mail Orders: PO Box 2980
Sacramento, CA 95812-2980

National Ocean Service
Distribution Branch (N/cg33)
Riverdale, MD 20737-1199
(301) 436-6990
NOS and DMA nautical and aeronautical charts; telephone orders accepted.

Shkurkin, Vlad
6025 Rose Arbor Avenue
San Pablo, CA 94806
(415) 232-7742
Microfilm and prints of Sanborn and other fire insurance maps of cities.

Tradewind Instrument, Ltd.
2540 Blanding Avenue
Alameda, CA 94501
(510) 523-5726
NOS, DMA and British Admiralty nautical charts.

Read also *Magazine & Booksellers of SF* and *Little Libraries & Museums* for more map sources in San Francisco. We have a list of antiquarian and out-of-print map sellers and a guide to *Sanborn Insurance Maps*. Send us an SASE and we'll mail you a copy. Send to THE SAN FRANCISCO ALMANAC, *Map Hunt,* 1657 Waller Street #A, SF, CA 94117-2811 or call 1-800-352-5268.

Pioneer Society Museum & Library

Located at 456 McAllister, The Pioneer Society of California Museum (861-5278) displays an impressive array of vintage maps, most showing The City's downtown area back to the Gold Rush era. Open daily.

Still Waters Run Deep

We're hoping to reprint a book of maps that clearly indicates the location, flowrate and potability of 900 fresh water springs still flowing beneath The City. The source book of wells was researched and edited by famed City Engineer O'Shaughnessy in 1913, when pumps and wells still provided most water and Hetch Hetchy was yet to be.

Use of this H_2O would reduce use of the rare Hetch Hetchy water pumped from 100 miles away. The water still flows in hundreds of locations around SF (even beneath City Hall).

If you'd like a copy of this rare book of maps, call or send a postcard expressing your interest. We'll let you know when it will be available.

Vanished Waters

San Francisco is a town built where no city should ever have been. The SF peninsula arose from the sea just 10,000 years ago; it was a marshy beach with a few shale hills when the pioneers arrived in 1849. Even the local native Indians preferred Oakland to "Yerba Buena." On top of everything, this now-filled marshland sits between two of the most active plate-faults, the San Andreas and Hayward.

Vanished Waters, a book written and published by Nancy Olmsted and the Mission Creek Conservancy, is the story of the transformation of San Francisco from marsh and swamp lands. It is a fascinating tale of mystery and intrigue and is chock-full of historic photos and maps of The Mission and South of Market areas from SF's developmental years 1849–1890 through the 20th Century. Tales of political antics and short-sighted land programs would be purely humorous, if not for the terrible impact these past follies have had on the ecology of the Bay's wetlands and the future of The City, now poised on the brink of predicted devastation by earthquake and/or resulting fire.

Vanished Waters *is available at Cody's Books in Berkeley and at Green Apple Books. List price, $15.00. If you hold an interest in SF history, this book is most highly recommended.*

Little Libraries & Museums

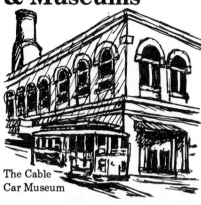

The Cable Car Museum

Here's a selection of perhaps smaller and perhaps somewhat less-known local libraries and museums that may be able to help you in your pursuit of the past, present or future.

Many, such as the Shaw Maritime Library, are anything but small, but spend much less of their budgets on outreach than larger institutions.

Public-use hours are often limited and change frequently with budget realities. Call the library of your choice before you visit.

Watch for reviews of more fine local libraries and museums in our newsletter, *The Almanac News.* (Many are listed at the end of this section.)

The Boxing Museum

Civic Auditorium, 99 Grove Street
Take elevator to Third Floor
Free admission

San Francisco was once known as "The Boxing Capitol of the World." It was a wide-open city, and attracted the battling kind from many cities and countries around the world. Many of boxing's favored sons hailed from San Francisco, including middleweight Fred Apostoli (who grew up in North Beach). That tradition has continued to the present-day, with the emergence of junior-middleweight challenger "Irish" Pat Lawlor, "The Pride of the Sunset."

A smartly designed exhibit highlights one of the milestones in the history of "the sweet science" when, on Sept. 7, 1892, City Hall accountant–bank teller "Gentleman" Jim Corbett triumphed over John L. Sullivan in 21 rounds.

The Boxing Museum was created by Wendy Helder and her associates and many local boxing fans. The museum fills a hallway on the third floor of the Civic Auditorium and is a sincere tribute to the sport, its players and San Francisco's central role. Great old photographs, boxing magazines, gloves and trophies are on display. One of SF's smallest, least visited and most interesting museums. Recommended.

Cable Car Museum

Did you know that at one time the cable car was used in 28 other cities around the world, including Butte, Montana; Seattle; Edinburgh, Scotland and Washington, DC? This working museum takes us into the belly-of-the-beast itself—the cable car powerhouse.

The red masonry powerhouse, constructed in 1907, supplies the power that keeps miles of steel cable running beneath the streets. The museum provides clear views of the system at work and offers numerous fun and informative exhibits to capture the history and evolution of the cable cars.

The Cable Car Museum allows us to learn how the system really works. Giant electric motors and a mammoth configuration of cables, sheaves and pulleys pull together, along with an army of cable car operators and skilled service persons, to operate these roving goodwill ambassadors.

Operated in fine fashion by the Pacific Coast Chapter of the Railway and Locomotive Historical Society, the Cable Car Museum is located at Washington and Mason Streets at the foot of Nob Hill and is open daily from 10 a.m. - 5 p.m.

The museum gift shop carries many great books about the cable cars and is a must-stop for your Holiday shopping. Call 474-1887.

California Historical Society

2099 Pacific Avenue (at Baker)
567-1848
Open to the Public
Wednesdays 10 a.m. - 4 p.m.

The California Historical Society is dedicated to collecting, preserving and interpreting history and information about California and the West. The City, of course, is the central player in the developing Western United States; simply put, this is where it all started.

The library and archives hold by far the world's largest collection of materials about the history of California and San Francisco. There are 35,000 books, 3,700 maps and hundreds of thousands of pamphlets, posters and ephemera. The renowned picture collection consists of nearly a half-million photographs. There are 8,500 manuscripts and letters penned by SF notables including Adolph Sutro, Bret Harte, "Emperor" Norton and others. Over ten million *San Francisco Chronicle* newspaper clippings are on file!

It's a closed stack, meaning that you must locate the item in the index and the staff librarian will retrieve it. You will be given a pair of white cotton gloves, with only pencils allowed for note-taking. It's this special care that allows each item to last through the centuries. There is a $5.00 per visit fee, which helps the library to continue to serve us all. Memberships available.

The City Hall Library: SF's Hall of Records

We weren't sure where to put the vital Hall of Records, so we've included it here. If you're researching a building's history, this is your first stop. Here you can locate the building's block and parcel numbers, e.g., 1251—20, which is how The City keeps track of its lots and buildings. There are numerous research sources available, including the Real Property Index on microfilm and the huge map/plat books, if you're going back a few years. (You will find few pre-1906 records.) This is where real property transfers are recorded. In this room you'll also find marriage records, birth and death records, records of tax liens, health violations and more. Copies are available of microfilm and microfiche indexes for about $1.00 a page. The staff can be very helpful. The Hall of Records is in The Recorder's Office, Room 167 at City Hall, weekdays 8:30 a.m. - 4:30 p.m.

County Clerk's Office

Room 317, City Hall. Computer and hard-copy information about fictitious business names, lawsuits and more. Hard copies can be ordered or done on the spot, if there are five pages or fewer. This place is always teeming with lawyers! Open 8:30 a.m. - 4:30 p.m. Copies about 50¢/page.

Fire Department Museum

The history of San Francisco is written in the ashes of her many fires. To honor the bravery of those who risked their lives to put out the fires, a group of citizens and firefighters formed the Saint Francis Hook and Ladder Society—sponsors of the SFFD Museum—in 1973. The fire station/museum is located at Presidio Avenue between Bush and Pine and is open Thursday-Sunday, 1 p.m. - 4 p.m.

The museum features one of the largest collections of fire-fighting artifacts, appartus and memorabilia in the West. Tank Wagon Company No. 7, a 1937 Fageol pumper, is a show-stopper. An 1897 La France Steam Pumper is an impressive apparatus, too. If you have an interest in SF's past and future, plan a visit to this quiet little museum. It is recommended that you call before you visit, as volunteers are not always available to staff the museum. Call 861-8000, ext. 365. (Volunteers are always in demand if you can help.)

While you're there, purchase "Tour of San Francisco Firehouses." This $5.00 guide is a handy reference to SF's existing historic fire stations, some dating back to the 1890s. You can also take City Guides' free walking tour. Call City Guides at 557-4266.

Jewish Community Library

639 14th Avenue
(at Balboa in The Richmond)
751-6983
Sun., Mon.,Wed. 10 a.m. - 4 p.m.
Tues. Noon - 6 p.m.
Thurs. Noon - 8 p.m.

Housed within a beautiful 1920s mansion, this rich library offers over 27,000 volumes: books, magazines, videotapes and newsletters and newspapers devoted to Judaica.

This modern facility (opened in 1977) reflects on a broad-based spectrum of issues and writers, shedding light on questions addressed by Jews all over the world. Religion, art, music (there are scores, recordings and a music room), history and popular writings are well-indexed in a bright, relaxed facility with a most helpful staff. The reading room is perfect for relaxed contemplation. The library welcomes the community, with lending privileges extended to anyone with a valid ID.

The adjoining Tibor Havas and Anton Ajtai Children's Library is a special treasure for parents, too. Also located in the building is The Holocaust Center of Northern California (751-6041). The two libraries are sponsored by the Bureau of Jewish Education, a national organization, and supported by Friends of the Jewish Community Library, volunteers and members.

Mechanics Institute

57 Post Street (by Market)
421-1768
Mon.-Thurs. 9 a.m. - 9 p.m.
Fri. 9 a.m. - 6 p.m.
Sat. 10 a.m. - 6 p.m.
Sun. 1 p.m. - 5 p.m.

This is the oldest and one of the best general interest libraries in The City. Begun in 1855, it merged with The Mercantile Library after the 1906 earthquake. Today, it houses over 200,000 volumes, including books, tapes and ephemera. It is one of the best sources for local history in SF.

This posh private library is all yours for a $45.00 annual membership fee. Regular researchers will find the cost very reasonable for the vast banks of knowledge available, the excellent indexing and the superb facilities. Look for fiction, biographies, history, travel, science, math, technology, religion, art, music and more. There is a great deal of material on business, including a newspaper clip file and a collection of annual reports. Two reference librarians are available at all times and the library offers the best hours in town.

To help you make a decision as to whether to join the Institute, free orientation tours are held each Wednesday at noon, meeting at the third floor desk. A fine opportunity for San Franciscans who do research regularly.

Museum of the City and County of San Francisco

The Cannery/Leavenworth & Bay
928-0289
Wed.-Sun. 11 a.m. - 4 p.m.

Talented former City Archivist Gladys Hansen and her historian son Richard Hansen opened this eye-opening museum in 1991. This one-room museum has a message with a big impact: If San Francisco cannot learn from her past, specifically the 1906 earthquake and fire, then she is doomed to repeat it.

Exhibits in this museum clearly demonstrate the terrible devastation to buildings, property and life and limb that the 1906 conflagration brought to bear. The exhibits also suggest the possibility of an even more devastating scenario in the "Big One" just ahead. The Hansens' own research has pointed up numerous illuminating facts. For example, many more deaths occurred than stated by City newspapers and City Hall at the time. This indicates that the 8.3 quake that lasted eighty seconds did damage that was later attributed to the fire.

Look for maps, old photographs, quake artifacts and more. The Hansens have received the entire Raymond Clary collection, which they hope to make more accessible to the public in the decade ahead. To contribute your resources, do call. Recommended.

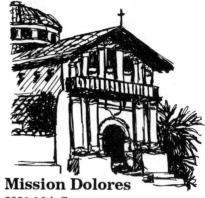

Mission Dolores

3321 16th Street
Call 621-8203 for tour appointments.
10 a.m. - 4 p.m. Daily

Mission Dolores was built in 1791. The adobe mission building is SF's oldest standing structure and is well worth a self-tour, or better, the Mission tour given daily. (The adjoining Parish Church, at the corner of Dolores and 16th Street, did not survive the 1906 earthquake, as did the adobe mission building.)

The cemetery in the rear is fascinating. Many of San Francisco's prominent first citizens were buried at Mission Dolores, as well as a few of the most notorious. Note the large number of Irish families buried in this cemetery in the difficult post-Gold Rush years. There is also a small museum devoted to SF's earliest days.

Mission Dolores gave rise to the career of a Mission District gardener and carpenter, Harry Downie. From doing handywork at the aging Mission as a teenager, he spent his entire life restoring many of California's original 21 missions founded by Father Junipero Serra. Eventually he was buried within the basilica of his favorite project, the mission in Carmel.

Nautical Research Centre Library

Many of our best "little" libraries began as private collections, such as the Shaw Library, Sutro Library, SF PALM and others. Colin MacKenzie's Nautical Research Centre is a case in point. A public reference library, this fine resource at 335 Vallejo Street (in Petaluma) is dedicated to the world's lighthouses and life-saving stations.

Over 500 books and pamphlets have been catalogued, the largest single collection of materials about this important maritime subject. There is a color slide collection, audio materials, videos and lots of related ephemera. Friendly librarian MacKenzie keeps clippings sent to him by lighthouse aficionados around the world on lighthouse projects, historical items and much more. Lighthouse and maritime researchers from the Bay Area and many far-away places write, call or visit this archive.

Sea artifacts, old maps and maritime curios are on display in the library building, built next to his home by friends and volunteers. This library is a well-catalogued tribute to the heroic men and women who ran the lighthouses and lightships for centuries, before being replaced by modern unmanned signals. Open Sun.–Fri. from 9 a.m. - 9 p.m. Call (707) 763-8453 for suggested appointments.

North Beach Museum

The North Beach Museum, upstairs at Eureka Federal Savings Bank at Columbus and Stockton, is worth a visit next time you're in North Beach or Chinatown. An eight-foot panoramic map of the bayfront from 1862 really conveys the village feeling of SF after The Gold Rush. An early hand-cranked foghorn and gold-laid vestments and chalice from Saint Peter & Paul's Church are among the many Italian and Chinese exhibits in this neighborhood tribute. Open during bank hours. Call 391-6210.

Old Mint Museum

This historic building is a treat for architecture lovers, a classic example of pre-earthquake design that thankfully survived the 1906 event. The Old Mint, which once employed California writer Bret Harte, offers a fine reminder of the rich post-Gold and Silver Rush years. Tours are offered daily. Call 974-0788 for tour information.

Randall Museum

199 Museum Way
Call 554-9600 for directions

The Randall Museum is a Recreation and Parks project located atop Corona Heights. Children and parents share in a broad-based science, nature and history program featuring classroom hands-on activities and special nature and arts projects. Permanent science, evolutionary and animal exhibits are an educational treat.

There is a working seismograph and quake-map exhibit, registering even minor ground-shakes as many as 5,000 miles away. A dinosaur exhibit maps the growth of San Francisco through the epochs. An indoor zoo features ground animals, birds and reptiles. (Call for zoo hours.)

A beautiful shop, a small auditorium and bright, airy classrooms make the Randall Museum the perfect place for living and learning about the world around us. The view from up here, by the way, is tops!

The energetic staff and dedicated volunteers of Friends of the Randall Museum offer daily classes and workshops, which are the main thrust of this learn-by-doing workshop resource. To receive more info, call or visit. You'll be pleased to discover this one! (Volunteers always in demand, too.)

Presidio Museum

Presidio Drive, near Base Headquarters
Free admission; call 561-4115 for info.
Tues.-Sun., 10 a.m. - 4 p.m.

San Franciscans often forget just how beneficial the presence of the US Army at The Presidio has been. The Presidio Museum, directed by Herb Garcia, was established in 1973 to preserve the colorful history of those men and women who have guarded the Golden Gate for more than 200 years.

Located within a building that was built in 1857, the oldest standing building on the base, this charming museum offers exhibits on The Presidio's early Hispanic heritage, the 18th and 19th Centuries and the 1906 earthquake and fire. Old maps and photographs help us envision the military's role in San Francisco. The City also played a major role in the two world wars. Other exhibits portray the 1915 Panama Pacific Exposition and turn-of-the-century Pacific expansion, among others. This fine little military museum should be visited by all. Follow the signs from any inroad to the museum.

When San Francisco burned to the ground in 1906, The Presidio served as refuge to thousands of City residents. Many lived in tents and refugee shacks, such as those on display here. Here at THE ALMANAC, *we're a little concerned about what'll happen next time, when The Presidio and the Army are gone...*

San Francisco History Room

SF Main Library, Third Floor
557-4567
Tues. & Fri. Noon - 6 p.m.
Wed. 1 p.m. - 6 p.m.
Thurs. & Sat. 10 a.m. - 6 p.m.

The San Francisco History Room offers SF's widest range of local history references and special collections. It is a warm, quiet, charming place, lending itself to hours of enjoyable study.

There are 300,000 photographs, 40,000 color slides, hundreds of old guide books, neighborhood building surveys, maps and more to help you research your home, family, business or any other favorite San Francisco subject. The room includes a collection of fine press and rare books, including the Robert Grabhorn Collection, the Schmulowitz Collection of Wit and Humor, the Richard Harrison Calligraphy Collection and others.

Special Collections Manager Faun McInnis and a talented and helpful staff, along with energetic Friends' volunteers, are working hard to help see the San Francisco Room into the 21st Century. It is one of the most versatile, easily-accessed and in-depth SF history collections available anywhere. Recommended resource.

Too much to tell, drop by for a visit.

San Francisco Performing Arts Library & Museum

399 Grove Street (Hayes Valley)
Weekdays 10 a.m. - 5 p.m.
Sat. Noon - 4 p.m. (appt. suggested)
255-4800

Begun as a personal collection of dance, art and design materials by an SF artist and dancer, Russell Hartley (1922-1983), this non-profit museum and archive captures the history of dance, theatre and opera in The City.

SF PALM began as Archives for the Performing Arts, the official archive of the San Francisco Opera, Ballet and Symphony, as well as for other arts institutions in The City. Today, it continues to expand, archiving today's creative works and continuing to preserve and index materials dating back to The Gold Rush. The collection includes 119 personal arts scrapbooks collected by Hartley, 6,000 books on the arts and a growing video and photo, artifacts and costumes collection. SF PALM offers anyone with an interest in the history of dance and theatre a precious closed-stacks resource, with a helpful staff available to give you access to it all.

If you can offer resources or time, or wish to become a member of this growing non-profit treasure trove of the arts, call SF PALM. (The group is currently planning to relocate to a bigger space!)

J. Porter Shaw Library

San Francisco Maritime Park
Fort Mason Bldg. E, Third Floor
556-9870
Tues. 5 p.m. - 8 p.m.
Wed.-Fri. 1 p.m. - 5 p.m.
Sat. 10 a.m. - 5 p.m.

This is the Pacific Coast's largest and pre-eminent library of commercial maritime history, focusing on sail and steam from 1520 to the present. The library holdings include over 15,000 volumes, as well as current and back-issues of 500 periodicals, covering the entire spectrum of maritime activity.

Ephemeral collections are comprised of 50,000 items in 2,500 subject groupings. The newspaper clipping library is large, with over 4 million citations referenced. Over 250,000 photographs! Vessel registers available include *Lloyd's*, *Record of American and Foreign Shipping* and *Merchant Vessels of the United States*, from 1764 to today.

Reference Librarian Irene Stachura showed us the modern facility, and impressed upon us the Shaw Library's extensive referencing. Much of this indexing was done these past twenty years under the direction of Principal Librarian David Hull. The ease of access to materials is astounding; free to public. Memberships are inexpensive and enriching. One of SF's best. *At publication the Shaw Library received a major whaling collection; inquire.*

Sutro Library

480 Winston Drive
(off Buckingham Drive,
behind Stonestown Mall)
731-4477
Weekdays 10 a.m. - 5 p.m.

The Sutro Library is a relatively unknown local treasure. Over the years, it has found its niche as a national resource for family histories, genealogy and local history. Over 40,000 titles include vital state birth, death, marriage and cemetery records; complete US census records from 1871–1910 (census records become public information after 70 years); directories from the Gold Rush era to the modern day and telephone books from around the world. Look for church histories, over 10,000 family histories, DAR lineage books, books and newsletters published by family heritage groups from all over the US and vast microfilm files.

The Sutro Library is a treat for local researchers: a comfortable, quiet, well-lit library offering interlibrary lending and reference, a most helpful staff and modern computer catalogues. If you are new to genealogy, there are numerous how-to books to help you get started in tracing your family tree.

This is the only branch of Sacramento's California State Library. Special thanks to Sutro Librarian Barbara Chambers for her help with this issue.

TREASURE ISLAND
M U S E U M

Treasure Island Museum

Open daily. Call 362-4473 for museum information.

Treasure Island was built of sand on the dangerous shoals of Yerba Buena Island. From these manmade beaches came the spectacular vision of the 20th Century—Treasure Island.

The Golden Gate Exposition opened on February 18, 1939. Its purpose was to celebrate the completion of the new Bay and Golden Gate Bridges and the peaceful partnership of the US, her Pacific Rim neighbors and the world. The Governor of California opened the lustrous gates of the glittering city with a key fashioned from California diamonds, tourmalines, benitoites and gold from across the nation.

The museum is an excellent reminder of that brief moment in history, between The Great Depression and World War II. Colorful exhibits, color films and hundreds of preserved items from the fair years 1939–1941 lead you into a US Navy exhibit about its role in WWII. A model of the 400-foot symbol of the fair, the Tower of the Sun, reminds us that its carillon bells now resound in Grace Cathedral. You'll meet Treasure Island "Theme Doll" Zoe Dell Lantis, who flew around the world to publicize the event aboard the Pan-Am China Clipper, the Concorde SST of its day.

Strybing Arboretum's Helen Russell Library

Strybing Arboretum
GG Park, by Ninth Ave. & Lincoln Way
661-1514
Daily 10 a.m. - 4 p.m. (Closed Holidays)

Dedicated in 1972, the Helen Crocker Russell Library is devoted to the literature of horticulture and related subjects, with particular emphasis on plants that can be grown in The City's very special Mediterranean climate.

The library contains more than 14,000 volumes and keeps on file over 300 magazines and newsletters published by clubs, societies and others. The library is an excellent reference for materials about garden design, landscaping, history of horticulture, gardening techniques and botanical illustration. There is an extensive collection of seed and nursery catalogues, a photo archive featuring GG Park, rare books and more.

This is a public (non-circulating) reference library with a Librarian available to help you—all in a beautiful Park setting!

More *Libraries & Museums*

Museo Italo Americano
673-2200

Holocaust Oral History Project
751-0659

Mills Law Library
781-2665

Alliance Francaise Library
775-7755

Goethe Institute Library
391-0428

Russian Cultural Museum
921-4082

Libreria Cristinia
431-9027

Libreria Mexico
647-0329

California Genealogical Society
777-9936

Sierra Club's William Colby Library
776-2211

Chinese Historical Museum
391-1188

Society of California Pioneers Museum
861-5278

African American Museum & Library
441-0640

Marion Center and Library
863-5373

Jewish Community Museum
543-8880

Octagon House
441-7512

Craft & Folk Art Museum
775-0990

Printing Industry of California
495-8242

Pacific Heritage Museum
399-1124

Japanese-American Library
567-5006

Gay & Lesbian Historical Society
626-0980

Mexican Museum
441-0404

Cartoon Art Museum
546-9481

Ansel Adams Center
495-7242

Museum of Ophthalmology
561-8500

Children's Multicultural Center
673-2197

See *Magazine and Booksellers, Maps and Map Sellers, Almanac Green* and other chapters in this ALMANAC for more information sources in The City.

Federal Reserve Bank of SF Library
974-3216

Schmidt Medical Hospital Library
California College of Podiatric Medicine
563-3444

Pacific Gas & Electric Co. Library
973-2573

J.W. Maillard, Jr. Library
California Academy of Sciences
221-4214, Ext. 275

St. Mary's Medical Center Library
750-5784

San Francisco Art Institute Library
749-4559

Avery Brundage Collection Library
Asian Art Museum of San Francisco
668-8921

SF Conservatory of Music Library
564-8086

SF Chronicle Library
777-7230

SF Examiner Library
777-7845

Louise Ackerman Library
SF Museum of Modern Art
863-8800

Standard Oil Company Library
894-7700

UCSF Library
666-2334

Hastings College of Law Library
565-4750

Pacific Bell Telephone Museum
542-0182

Wells Fargo Museum & Library
399-7357 (Library)

City Hall
Hall of Records
County Clerk's Office

Many libraries and small museums require advance appointments or have limited public hours. Call the institution of your choice for hours, location and information.

If you know of a local resource that we may have missed, please do call or write so that we are able to include it in the next ALMANAC.

Our Public Library

Library Budget Crisis— Call to Action!

Cutting library budgets to curtail City spending is a short-sighted and highly negative financial policy. The citizens of a world-class city like San Francisco require the best public library system available to live bright, productive lives and to continue to learn and prosper as people and good citizens.

Join Friends of the Public Library. A small membership fee brings a mix of benefits and shows your support for a quality public library system in SF. Friends is lobbying hard for the cause. If the Friends envelope included in this ALMANAC didn't reach you, call Friends of the Public Library at 557-4257.

Keep the Libraries Alive! Join Friends of the Public Library Today! Call 557-4257.

Friends of the Public Library

Friends of the Public Library is a non-profit organization dedicated to the advancement of SF's public library system. It offers a wide range of special services and is supported by funding from membership donations and private and corporate funding.

Membership includes many special invitations to literary lectures and events, and much more. It also includes a special pass to the annual book sale's first day preview sale. If you want to be a part of this drive to make our library a better one and reap the rich fruits of membership, join Friends of the Public Library.

Bookmobile Really Real!

The bookmobile brings books to home-bound seniors at senior resident buildings in San Francisco. Call 557-4345 for bookmobile scheduling info. The new bookmobile will be ready in Summer 1992. (See *All Things SF.*)

Library Cards

Library cards are issued at The Main Library. A bill showing residence in SF and a City address driver's license or California ID is required. There is no charge for your borrower's card. Items are borrowed for 7–21 day loan periods. Fines equal 10¢ per day for each item overdue. If you lose or misplace your card, a replacement card can be received for a small fee.

Treat library loans as you would treat any valuable loan from a friend or family member. Books returned late, damaged or lost only hurt your neighbor borrower. Books lost or damaged will cost book value plus $5.00 for replacement. Records, videos and some other items may have shorter loan periods and different overdue fees. Ask at checkout if you're not sure.

Friends offers free adult tours of The Main Library at 200 Larkin. If you are new to the system, or want to know more about the main facility, this expert tour will prove invaluable. The one-hour tour will introduce you to the system and the card catalogue and help you find magazine and newspaper articles. Call Friends at 557-4257.

Main Library Telephone Numbers

Here's a list of frequently used telephone numbers for The Main Library at 200 Larkin Street. General information can provide extensions at 557-4400.

Art & Music	557-4525
Audio Visual	557-4515
Borrower, Return Info	557-4363
Business & Science	557-4488
Children's Room	557-4554
Circulation	557-4500
City Guides	
(Free Walking Tours)	557-4266
Community Relations	557-4277
Hearing Impaired Services	
(TDD)	557-4433
(Voice)	557-4434
Friends of the Library	557-4257
General Information	**557-4400**
Government Materials	557-4488
Humanities	557-4545
Library Card Info.	557-4363
Municipal References	557-4444
Periodicals & Directories	557-4440
Personnel	557-4585
Project Read	557-4388
SF History Room	557-4567
Special Collections	557-4560

Call Friends to volunteer at 557-4257. People are needed to help with walking tours, the bookmobile and many other Friends endeavors. One of SF's most interesting and educational volunteer opportunities.

Project Read Volunteers

Project Read trains volunteers in tutoring English-speaking adults who want to learn to read. Volunteers commit for one year and tutor at least 90 minutes per week. A one-time tutor registration fee of $20 covers part of the cost of materials provided during the ten-hour basic training course. Continuing education and group events are held regularly. Call 557-4388.

The New Main Library: Coming Soon...

Ground was broken in May 1992 for the new Main Library! The much-needed facility, located between Fulton and Grove, will be built just across the street from the existing building, which was constructed in 1917. That building will be renovated and will become home to The Asian Art Museum.

Kids' Services

Storytime readings are held at many libraries. Branches give lap-sit programs for infants, toddlers and parents, as well as readings for tiny tots, ages 3–5. Call your local branch for program schedules.

Here are three great touch-tone storytellers for kids. They're free!

Dial-a-Story for Ages 3–5	626-6516
Dial-a-Story (Spanish)	552-0535
Dial-a-Story (Cantonese)	552-0534

Summer reading programs and other activities for kids are available.

Our new Main Library will have six above-ground floors and a basement. The library will offer 190,000 linear feet of stacks. (That's 36 miles of books!)

Besides more room for books, the new Main Library will include computerized catalogues, on-line data access for homes and offices, a bookstore and much more. Regular users of 200 Larkin are eagerly awaiting the opening of this beautiful facility, scheduled for late 1995.

To find out more about this entire joyous matter, visit 200 Larkin, where you can look at a scale model of the new facility or pick up a pamphlet called *The New Main*.

Branch/Reading Libraries

Last year we included hours of operation of each branch. Today, with branches facing imminent cutbacks due to City budget decisions, we have not done so. Get involved. Join Friends of the Public Library, and tell City Hall that our public libraries *must* receive full funding. Join Friends, today!

Main Library
Mon., Wed., Thurs, Sat. 10 a.m. - 6 p.m.
Tues. Noon - 9 p.m.
Fri. Noon - 6 p.m.
Closed Sunday
Call for revised hours;
Main Phone Number: 557-4400.

Anza
550 37th Ave.   666-7160

Bayview—Anna E. Waden
5075 3rd Street   468-1323

Bernal Heights
500 Cortland Avenue   695-5160

Chinatown
1135 Powell Street   274-0275

Eureka Valley/Harvey Milk Memorial
3555 16th Street   554-9445

Excelsior
4400 Mission Street   337-4735

Glen Park Reading Center
653 Chenery Street   337-4740

Golden Gate Valley Reading Center
1801 Green Street   292-2195

Ingleside Reading Center
387 Ashton Ave.   337-4745

Library for the Blind
3150 Sacramento Street   292-2022

Marina
1890 Chestnut Street   292-2150

Merced
155 Winston Drive   337-4780

Mission
3359 24th Street   695-5090

Noe Valley
451 Jersey Street   695-5095

North Beach
2000 Mason Street   274-0270

Ocean View Reading Center
111 Broad Street   337-4785

Ortega
3223 Ortega Street   753-7120

Park
1833 Page Street   666-7155

Parkside
1200 Taraval Street   753-7155

The San Francisco Room

Portola Reading Center
2434 San Bruno Ave.   468-2232

Tuesday & Friday, Noon - 6 p.m.
Wednesday, 1 p.m. - 6 p.m.
Thursday & Saturday, 10 a.m. - 6 p.m.

Potrero
1616 20th Street   285-3022

(Due to staff shortages, the room is sometimes closed between Noon and 1 p.m. Call 557-4567.)

Presidio Reading Center
3150 Sacramento St.   292-2155

Richmond
351 9th Avenue   666-7165

Folks discuss endlessly where to find the best view of San Francisco. Twin Peaks, Bernal Heights, Nob Hill; everyone has an opinion, sure as gold glitters. No view, however, offers the timeless vista of The San Francisco Room at The Main Library. All the past folly and endeavor of San Francisco can be rediscovered here.

Sunset (temporarily closed)
1305 18th Avenue   753-7130

Visitacion Valley Reading Center
45 Leland Avenue   337-4790

West Portal
190 Lenox Way   753-7135

The room has particular material handling rules. A guidesheet is available. The special care allows these works to shine the light that history's lamp holds to our present day, and to our always uncertain future. Nowhere is so much wonderful San Francisco history available to the public, free.

Western Addition
1550 Scott Street   292-2160

(See *Little Libraries & Museums*.)

The existing Main Public Library was designed by George Kelham and opened in 1918. It is built in the Italian Renaissance style. Carved inscriptions can be found throughout. One reads: *Books are the basis of civilized life and the fountains in the desert of being.*

Bookstore by the Bay

The Book Bay at Fort Mason Center, Building C, offers many bargain books, records and tapes donated to The Friends of the San Francisco Public Library. It is a pleasant little used bookstore often filled with rare finds! Book donations are welcome, too. Call 771-1076 for donation and bookstore information. If you have three boxes or more to donate, call 557-4257 for home book pick-up. Open Wed.-Fri. from 11-5, Thurs. 11-8 and Sat.-Sun. 11-5.

Big Annual Book Sale

The annual book sale at Fort Mason Center takes place in late May or early June. Fifty-thousand titles are laid out upon row after row of tables; they are priced to move fast. The first day of this event is a "preview" sale. It's a singular thrill to rush with the throngs into this arena and come up with a box of hardbacks. (Bring a box or two.)

Call Friends of the Public Library at 557-4257 for more information. A basic membership in Friends includes admission to the first day of the sale, which is *the* way to go if you plan to attend. (Other days are free.) The sale runs for four days, and all items are half-price the last day. On opening day there is a silent auction of the rare and unusual, including *objets d'art,* stamp collections and collages. See you there!

San Francisco's *Business Directories* 1877-1982

These thick annual tomes were the early equivalent of the *Yellow Pages,* chock full of information about stores, services and much more. These City volumes, published by Polk, Crocker and Langley, are displayed in the Periodicals Room of the Main Library.

Everyone who was anyone was listed! If a customer had a complaint with your service, you had better watch out. The *Business Directories* included the home addresses of business owners and employees, and listed their home telephone numbers, too! (Note the lack of a 1906 directory.)

In light of recent City budget deliberations that may have a negative effect on library funding, we have included the Friends of the Public Library's membership envelope in this ALMANAC. This helps Friends to lobby for proper library funding. Other benefits of membership include a host of events and programs and a great newsletter. If you didn't receive your Friends membership envelope, call Friends of the Public Library at 557-4257 to receive one by mail.

Cups

a cafe journal

Coffee Break with *CUPS*

"A cup of coffee is a miracle."

—Heinrich Eduard Jacob

The Cafe Tradition

To trace the origins of San Francisco's unique cafe tradition is to travel a path marked by a fascinating history of commerce, culture, religion and politics.

Ever since the stimulating properties of the bitter green bean were first discovered by the Ethiopians, coffee—the beverage and the culture that surrounds it—has provoked passion, controversy, change, repression and revolution.

In northern Africa and the Arab countries, the coffeehouse as we know it today was conceived and established as a center for conversation, music, storytelling and art. In 1511, the governor of Mecca attempted to repress coffeehouses, "for in these places men and women meet and play violins, tambourines, chess and do other things contrary to our sacred law."

Similar repressions followed in Cairo, and in 1606 the Grand Vizier of Constantinople ordered coffeehouses closed, saying that they "encouraged sedition." The first time one was caught drinking an illegal cup of coffee, he was to be beaten with a stick; the second time, sewn in a leather bag and dumped in the Bosphorous.

The wily purveyors of the brew were not easily discouraged, however. Floating coffeehouses developed, as people with pots made espressos in alleys and behind buildings. Soon the beverage was on its way to Europe, via Turkey and Greece.

A traveler's journal from 1664 relates the scene at one Turkish coffeehouse where "guests remain in the fresh air and amuse themselves watching passers-by," listening to music, reading and, of course, drinking thick, rich coffee.

The Turks acknowledged the intense mental and intellectual atmosphere of the coffeehouses, calling them the "schools of the wise." Likewise, the English referred to their coffeehouses as "penny universities." For the price of a newspaper (one penny—coffee cost two pence, including the paper) one could participate in a floating seminar that might include the likes of Addison and Steele.

Coffeehouses spread rapidly throughout England, and became central to intellectual, social and commercial life. In London alone, more than 2,000 cafes were in operation by the late 17th Century, which led to another attempt by the government to eliminate the bothersome brew.

In 1675 King Charles II of England published an edict closing the coffeehouses, his response to "The Women's Petition against Coffee," in which the authors contended that coffee drinking had made their husbands "as unfruitful as the deserts, from whence that unhappy berry is said to be brought." As a result, they argued, "the whole race is in danger of extinction."

Meanwhile, the bean was causing a commotion on the continent, attracting the attention of the Vatican. The clergy appealed to Pope Clement VIII to ban the brew, calling it the "devil's drink." The Pope, however, enjoyed java so much he decided to baptize it, thus "fooling Satan and making it a truly Christian beverage."

Cafes in Italy proliferated, and the flavor of these 17th-Century Italian cafes came to San Francisco in the 1950s, when Trieste-born Gianni Giotta arrived in North Beach. He opened Caffe Trieste, which served as the center for the Beat Generation and is still a favorite gathering place for poets, prophets and travelers.

Today, the cafe tradition in San Francisco is thriving. In fact, it's never been more alive than it is right now. From North Beach to the Mission to the Avenues, and even in the Financial District, cafes are one of the fastest growing businesses of the '90s. There are more than 150 cafes in The City today. Besides serving up some of the best coffee to be found anywhere in the world, many establishments also offer their patrons exhibits of local artists and photographers, live music, poetry readings...even bellydancing, story-telling and performance art.

One of the best ways to sample The City's cafes is by exploring individual neighborhoods. Mark Waldo, a Cafe Design Consultant who writes a column for *Cups*, emphasizes the importance of the cafe's connection with its neighborhood. He believes that good cafes reflect the character of the neighborhood and serve the community.

While North Beach is a favorite destination for tourists (Columbus Avenue offers some wonderful European-style cafes), other neighborhoods should be explored as well. The Mission District, from 16th to 24th Streets along Valencia Street, boasted more than fifteen cafes at last count. The neighborhood also has more bookstores per square mile than anywhere in the United States.

Hayes Valley, the Haight (Upper and Lower), South of Market (SOMA), Potrero Hill, Russian Hill, the Fillmore, the Castro, Noe Valley, Pacific Heights and the Avenues also merit serious sipping.

So grab your Muni pass and map, a blank notebook and that novel that's been sitting on your nightstand for months and get out there. There's a cafe just waiting for you ...

–Camille Stupar

A Cafe Tour of San Francisco

Caffe Barberini
229 Columbus Avenue
(415) 397-9771

Located just down the block from City Lights Bookstore in almost-Chinatown, on-the-way-to-downtown, Caffe Barberini serves up the finest cappuccino this side of Rome. Owner Salvatore Fadda makes his own pastries and pasta on the premises, and his skill at the espresso machine sets a new standard for coffee-lovers. Even visitors from Italy have been known to exclaim "Even in Rome I never had it so good!"

Caffe Puccini
411 Columbus Avenue
(415) 989-7033

Caffe Puccini, named after the opera composer, features a fine assortment of espresso drinks and pastries as well as a great view of the Columbus Avenue human parade. The atmosphere is comfortable and casual, although people in tuxes have been seen standing at the counter, and limos have been known to double park on the street for a latte to go. Many locals come here daily, and conversations in Italian are not uncommon. And the jukebox features—you guessed it—opera.

Simple Pleasures Cafe
36th & Balboa
(415) 387-4022

What a surprise to come across this gem of a java joint way out here in the Avenues. Owner Sandy Gold has created quite an oasis in this aptly named coffeehouse. The coffee is good and the ambiance as warm and funky and bohemian as it gets. Live acoustic music performances on weeknights; see improvpisational comedy troupe Metropolis every other Saturday at 8 p.m. Comfortable tables and chairs, a few over-stuffed sofas and coffee-tables make this a coffeehouse lover's dream.

Exit Cafe
1777 Steiner (at Sutter)
(415) 929-7117

A laid-back, yet uptown, cafe located just two blocks from the Kabuki Theater, Exit Cafe features great food, perfect lattes and one of the finest poetry readings in this city of poets (Tuesdays at 7:30 p.m.) Owner/operator John Schtakleff has worked wonders with this space: impressive floor-to-ceiling graphics, warm earth tones and a couple of cozy corners. Live jazz and other events are held many evenings. Talk about the movie with friends over a luscious latte or glass of wine or beer, and have a snack—the sandwiches are made with fresh foccaccia. A delightful respite from the action of Fillmore Street.

Farley's
1315 18th Street
(415) 648-1545

One of the top ten cafes in the world. 'Nuf said.

Cafe Picaro
3120 16th Street
(415) 431-4089

The Mission District, or "The New Bohemia" as it's been called by some cultural commentators of late, is known for its bookstores and cafes. Cafe Picaro is a perfect place to explore both—it's located right next door to Adobe Books and boasts quite a library of its own.

Le Petit Cafe
2164 Larkin Street (at Green)
(415) 776-5356

For some of the finest pastries in town, try this cafe on Russian Hill. A neighborhood landmark—the crowd is as diverse and ever-changing as the area itself. Mornings and afternoons find lines of hang-abouts and ties putting in their orders at the counter.

Dinners from the kitchen of Bob and Maria Drake are served at candle-lit tables. Sunday brunch is justifiably popular. Wood floors and tables with bud vases, friendly and helpful waitpersons and the soft sunlight from tree-lined streets make this an intimate and inviting place to spend one morning or three hundred.

Java Bay Coffee Co.
2056 Chestnut Street
(415) 922-JAVA

One of the most popular neighborhood meeting places, Java Bay is an example of owner James Parker's ability to turn the ordinary into a unique and memorable experience. The look is California industrial, where palm trees, neon and MTV blend with corrugated steel. Counter windows open on warm days, and bar stools along the front of the store provide an unparalleled vantage point for people-watching on the main street of the Marina. Pick up some beans (they do their own roasting) or one of the many espresso drinks at this cafe. Java Bay is featured on the front and back covers of David Charles' book *California Espresso,* which features 113 coffee stops from San Diego to Lake Tahoe.

Spike's Cafe
139 8th Street (at Minna)
(415) 255-1392

Just South of Market, Spike's Cafe is one of those unique spots where SOMA types, students, professionals, bikers, rockers and artistes can come together to eat, dance, sip coffee or read comic books. Spike's features a restaurant and cafe upstairs. The coffee is good. The food is good. The prices are reasonable. There's a bar downstairs with live music in the evenings and dancing. What more could anyone want or need? Try it.

San Francisco Art Institute Cafe
800 Chestnut Street
(415) 749-4567

There's an energy here unlike any other in The City—the creative, bohemian, smell-of-oil-paint-thinner sound of Artists-discussing-Art energy that an art school fosters. As if that weren't enough, the view of the Bay and Coit Tower will bring you back again and again. Stroll the shaded alcoves and savor the etchings, photos, paintings, sculptures, drawings and sketches before heading back toward the cafe. Sit outside and catch a few rays as you sip your cappuccino or soda water.

Dottie's True Blue Cafe
522 Jones Street
(415) 885-2767

Exceptional service and hospitality here in the Tenderloin, as owners Stefen and Salvatore serve up some tasty breakfasts at a price that's right. This is one of the friendliest spots in The City, a mix of regulars and tourists who can talk around the counter or from table to table. Everyone will feel right at home in this blue and white checkered tablecloth, downhome diner/cafe. Postcards on the wall from customers past and present attest to the impression these guys make. They're also very active in the local community, putting on a monthly benefit dinner for various causes 'round town; call for details. Or better yet, stop in for breakfast or lunch.

Mad Magda's Russian Tea Room & Cafe
579 Hayes Street
(415) 864-7654

Smoking da, or smoking nyet? A Rasputin sandwich or Chekhov salad? A warm and whimsical cafe, with wonderful colors and charming touches such as the 3-D domes of St. Basil's on the wall and a magic garden out back, Mad Magda's serves up coffee, light meals, pastries and tea with fun and imagination. Tarot, palm and tea leaf readings available after noon, and a variety of events including "Tina's No-Tech Low-Tech 45 rpm Party" on Sundays. Call the cafe for details.

Cafe Francisco
2161 Powell Street
(415) 397-8010

A quiet and friendly spot located between North Beach and Fisherman's Wharf, Cafe Francisco is one of those places that feels familiar and fits comfortably in your first visit. An assortment of espresso drinks and teas are available for the thirsty traveler. Owner Mamoush and manager Christina also make wonderful soups and salads, best enjoyed in a cozy booth with friends or at one of the small, round tables that catch the morning sun. The cafe features monthly poetry readings and exhibits by local artists and occasional musical performances.

Toy Boat Dessert Cafe
Clement at Fifth
(415) 751-7505

An unexpected treat in this busy neighborhood of Chinese restaurants and discount stores, the Toy Boat is a pleasant place to meet friends or just take a break from a day of Clement Street shopping. Coffees, Italian sodas, ice cream and a variety of cookies and pastries are served. The warm and easy atmosphere and corner location and large windows make for perfect people-watching, and the playful interior is a nice change of pace. The Toy Boat is the ideal spot for perusing a book from Green Apple Books across the street or the liner notes from a LP or CD from one of the nearby shops.

Cafe Vocabulary

A few of The City's most popular coffee drinks:

espresso: a shot of coffee, strong and pure, made by spraying steam through ground coffee beans.

doppio *(dopey-o)*: a double ("A doppio cappuccino, please.")

macchiato *(mahk-kee-ah-to)*: espresso topped with just a dollop of foamed milk.

cappuccino *(cap-pu-chee-no)*: espresso with a thick layer of foam.

caffe latte *(lah-tay)*: espresso with steamed milk.

mocha *(moke-ah)*: espresso, chocolate with steamed milk, usually served with whipped cream.

red eye: a cup of house coffee mixed with a shot of espresso.

Cheers!

Enjoy your next cup with

Cups, a cafe journal

A monthly publication whose goal is to explore and enhance cafe life in San Francisco and beyond, *Cups* features reviews of cafes, local and distant; stories about the cafe experience; coffee architecture, literature and events; fiction; cartoons; poetry; columns on classic films, music and books; profiles of artists whose works are exhibited in local cafes; a monthly calendar called *Cafe Happenings;* a monthly crossword puzzle and more!

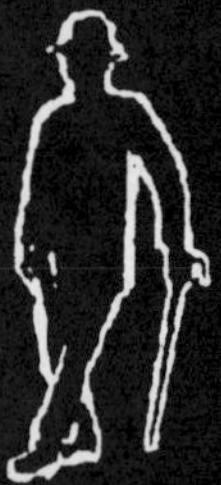

Now available in over 90 Bay Area cafes, from The Mission to The Avenues, Potrero Hill to North Beach. From out of town? Subscriptions available, one year (12 issues) for $20.00. Submissions accepted. Send SASE for return.

For more information call (415) 346-8194 or write:

Cups, a cafe journal
PO Box 471912
San Francisco, CA 94147-1912

Special thanks to *CUPS* Editor Camille Stupar for *Coffee Break*, a brand new ALMANAC feature. Look for *CUPS* at your local cafe, or better yet, subscribe by mail. One of The City's favorite periodicals!

Foghorns & Sea Knots

Balclutha

Maritime Museum at Aquatic Park

The Art Deco steel and glass upper deck of the SF Maritime Museum at Aquatic Park offers a sweeping view of the Bay, remarkably unchanged since The City's great maritime days. Photographs, artifacts and incredible ship models capture the essence of the days of exploration and expansion in SF and on the west coast. Halls document the Gold Rush, Cape Horn sailing vessels, the whaling industry and SF's important military past.

The building was dedicated in 1938. The project had been begun in 1931 through the combined efforts of City Hall, the WPA and private interests. It was built to serve as Aquatic Park's public bath house, housing a fully-equipped hospital, shower and locker rooms for 5,000 citizens, a full-service restaurant and the 2,000-seat exterior stairs, or spectator "stadia." The top-story penthouse held the public address system and announcer's office. Federal Arts Project muralist Hilaire Hiler, tile artist Sargent Claude Johnson, painter Richard Ayer and SF sculptor Beniamino Bufano created the Art Deco terrazzo floors, wall murals and sculptures to represent the wonder and mystery of the sea around us. Open daily, call 556-3002 for information.

The Maritime Bookstore

This rich bookstore sells books, maps, charts and ships-in-bottles. Although designed primarily to offer visitors gift books and maritime souvenirs, it also carries an impressive range of titles you won't likely find anywhere else.

While you're there, if you're as intrigued by the Maritime Museum building as we were, purchase *A Dream of Seven Decades: San Francisco's Aquatic Park,* written by James P. Delgado.

Parents will be pleased with the children's section, well-stocked with toys and books. The shop is located at the entrance to Hyde Street Pier, open daily 10 a.m. - 4 p.m. Call 775-BOOK. One of SF's best specialty bookshops; proceeds support maritime programs.

The Maritime Museum seeks volunteers in all areas: the small boat shop, shipwork, with collections, the library (see *Little Libraries*), photos and in the exhibit shop. The docent program needs people for public contact. Call 556-8545 for information.

Paddle-Wheel Steam Ferry *Eureka*

The *Eureka* was built in 1890 in Tiburon as a freight-car ferry and was christened *Ukiah*. After World War I she was overhauled. Her overhaul became so extensive that workers joked "we jacked up her whistle and slid a new boat underneath." In 1923 she became a passenger and automotive ferry and was re-named *Eureka*.

She continued in service until 1957 when her massive single-piston engine's connecting rod snapped. In her day she made the choppy voyage from Sausalito to SF's Ferry Building in 30 minutes. *Eureka* carried 2,300 passengers and 120 cars and trucks and offered commuting passengers comfortable seating, a cafe and even a magazine stand. Today *Eureka* still offers vintage vehicles and period magazines. You can almost smell the cigar smoke of bygone days. Tours are offered daily at 1:30 p.m. Call 556-3002.

Hyde Street Pier

The Hyde Street Pier slips prime examples of San Francisco's glorious days of the sea. Pay a small pier admission of $3.00 and spend an entire afternoon visiting the handsome lumber schooner *C.A. Thayer*, the square rigger *Balclutha*, the paddle tug *Eppleton Hall* and one of SF's greatest pre-bridge commuter ferries, the paddle-wheel ferry *Eureka*.

The Ferryboat *Eureka*

The Bay Lighthouses: Point Bonita

Point Bonita is a steep and perilous formation of grey rock that extends for one-half mile off the Marin Headlands. It forms the northern reaches of the narrow Golden Gate. In March 1853, Congress voted $25,000 to build a lighthouse and equip it with a French fresnel lens. Today this lens still serves as a beacon to navigators.

In haste, and with little West Coast lighthouse experience to fall back on, the first lighthouse was built at the highest point, 260 feet above the sea. The dense fog at such a height blocked the light. A "fog cannon" was added, fired on the hour and half-hour, the first of dozens of variations of the audible warning devices that later became commonplace as navigation aids, including foghorns, bells and whistles. In 1877, after much difficult tunnel-digging and foundation work, a new lighthouse was located on a lower cliff. A modern steam-driven fog trumpet, 16-feet-long, replaced the cantankerous and difficult-to-hear cannon. A rope-bridge, modeled after the Golden Gate Bridge, was built later to serve as the keeper's dwelling.

Many of the features of the past remain today, including the popular trail to the point, the winds, the crashing sea, the Coast Guard boathouse marine railway, the wind-dwarfed vegetation, the cave-tunnel and the beautiful fog-signal building and lighthouse. *Motorland Magazine* once called Point Bonita "the most magnificent setting of any lighthouse in the country." Call the Marin Headlands Visitor Center at 331-1540 for information about occasional tours conducted by knowledgable park guides.

San Rafael school teacher Ralph Shanks and his wife Lisa are maritime historians. Ralph was trained at California lighthouses since age eight, and is an active leader of the lighthouse and lifeboat preservation effort. His third book, *Guardians of the Golden Gate: Lighthouses and Lifeboat Stations of San Francisco Bay,* is immensely rich with history, humor and a deep-seated love and admiration for lighthouses and the people who manned them. It is available at The Maritime Store at Hyde Street Pier in paperback for just $14.95. Excellent book—a must-read.

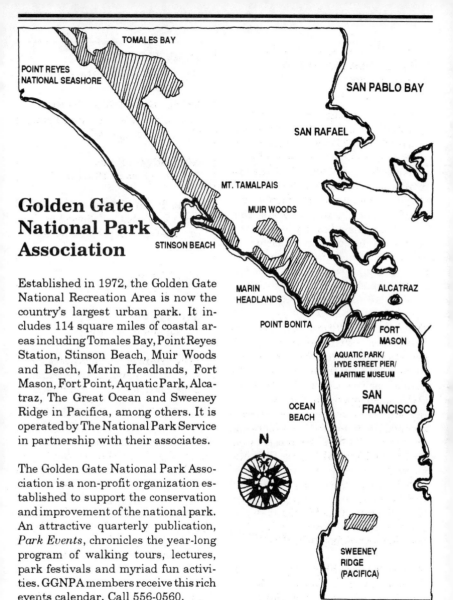

Golden Gate National Park Association

Established in 1972, the Golden Gate National Recreation Area is now the country's largest urban park. It includes 114 square miles of coastal areas including Tomales Bay, Point Reyes Station, Stinson Beach, Muir Woods and Beach, Marin Headlands, Fort Mason, Fort Point, Aquatic Park, Alcatraz, The Great Ocean and Sweeney Ridge in Pacifica, among others. It is operated by The National Park Service in partnership with their associates.

The Golden Gate National Park Association is a non-profit organization established to support the conservation and improvement of the national park. An attractive quarterly publication, *Park Events*, chronicles the year-long program of walking tours, lectures, park festivals and myriad fun activities. GGNPA members receive this rich events calendar. Call 556-0560.

The Grace Ships, 1869–1969

During its long history, Grace Line operated a number of vessels under charter from the US government. Two special Grace liberty ships are fondly remembered in San Francisco: the hospital vessel *HOPE* and the *Jeremiah O'Brien*. Former Grace purser William Kooiman, now a library technician at the Shaw Library at Fort Mason Center, has written a colorful and comprehensive history of the great fleet. Kooiman served nine years on *HOPE*, which sailed out the Golden Gate on her first tour of duty in 1960.

The *Jeremiah O'Brien*, now docked at Fort Mason, is the only surviving unaltered example of the 2,710 Grace ships rush-produced in the years 1941–1945. In her earliest years, the *Jeremiah O'Brien* shipped wartime cargo to Britain; later she was given special archival treatment by Grace Lines and finally, in 1978, by a local preservation group, the National Liberty Ship Memorial. Every May since 1980, she has sailed through the Golden Gate where floral wreaths are cast upon the sea to honor the men of the Merchant Marine and Naval Armed Guard, who lost their lives in our service during WWII.

Read The Grace Ships, 1869-1969, *by William Kooiman. Hardback $32.95. Available at The Maritime Store.*

FOG HORNS
Heard O'er The Bay

Golden Gate Bridge, Midspan: 1 sec. blast, 2 sec. silence, 1 sec. blast, 36 sec. silence*

GG Bridge, SF Pier: 2 sec. blast every 18 secs.*

Lime Point: 2 blasts every 30 secs.; 2 sec. blast, followed by 2 sec. silence, 2 sec. blast, 24 sec. silence

Point Diablo: 1 blast every 15 seconds

Mile Rock: 1 blast every 30 seconds

Point Bonita, 2 blasts every 30 secs.; 2 sec. blast, 2 sec. silence, 2 sec. blast, fol. by 36 sec. silence

* Thanks to Tom Andrade, Golden Gate Bridge Equipment Superintendent, for the fog signal info. He says that the old 250-lb. horns were replaced 10 years ago with even louder Wesley air whistles, which weigh only 45 lbs. The low tone you hear is the pier horns, the shriller tone comes from the midspan whistles. The whistles, heard up to six miles at sea, face east and west to serve all Gate traffic. The tone and interval have remained constant since the bridge was constructed, 1933–1937.

Palace of Fine Arts
Panama-Pacific International Exposition, 1915

Arts &
Music

Original Mural by *Mujeres Muralistas*

Mural Manifesto

The Precita Eyes Muralists was founded in 1977; they are a non-profit association of artists/muralists who offer walking tours of Mission murals every Saturday at 1:30 p.m. They also offer mural workshops and other art classes for adults and children. Classes are held at Precita Eyes Mural Arts Center, located at 348 Precita Avenue (just south of Army off Harrison).

Drop by Precita Mural Arts Center Monday-Friday 1 p.m. - 4 p.m. or Monday-Thursday 7:30 p.m. - 9:30 p.m. to buy a delightful mural map for a self-tour. Better yet, take a guided tour.

Learn more about the many fine murals that decorate The Mission and other neighborhoods in The City. Call 824-2810.

Film Arts Foundation

San Francisco's established independent filmmakers are well aware of the contribution of The Film Arts Foundation (FAF) to the SF arts scene. Since FAF was founded by a handful of filmmakers in 1976, it has grown to serve almost 2,000 members with a broad array of production resources and support services. Whether you are a filmmaker yourself, or like to watch new stars and directors on the rise, membership in FAF will keep you in touch with this vital Bay Area scene.

Membership in FAF brings you *Release Print,* the monthly newsletter that includes listings of festivals, funding resources and screening and broadcast opportunities in film and video. Their low-cost editing facility provides 16mm and Super-8 editing rooms, camera and lighting packages, a popular optical printer and sound transfers for members working on non-commercial film projects. There is a rich resource library, a viewing room, a group legal program, exhibitions, seminars, workshops and more.

The Film Society

Join the Film Society to support The SF International Film Festival and attend special screenings and previews all-year-long! The Festival is held each Spring at the fine Kabuki Theatres in Japantown. Call the Film Society at 567-4641 and ask them to send you a membership package.

Perhaps one of the best reasons to join FAF is to meet your fellow artists and share with them your resources, needs and project goals. Call FAF at 552-8760, or visit them at 346 9th Street for membership application and info.

Bravo String Quartet

Vladimir Venczel-Dimitrov and his wife Ildiko are half of one of San Francisco's newest and finest string quartets. Bravo String Quartet performed regularly for Governor Deukmejian's guests at The Governor's Mansion in Sacramento, before recently relocating to The City.

Quartet manager Vladimir began his lengthy career as a classical violist. He performed and trained throughout Europe before bringing his talents to sunny California. The Bravo String Quartet's repertoire includes over 60 hours of musical selections. They perform everything from the music of Bach to the Beatles, and everything that's in-between. The international range of their selection list is compelling. The tape they sent is an ALMANAC favorite!

Vladimir writes, "My wife Ildiko was accepted and has begun studies at UCSF. Now we are looking forward to being even more successful in this, the most beautiful City in the world."

Recommended group. Call The Bravo String Quartet and request their song list before planning your next special event. Speak to Vladimir at 731-6350.

San Francisco Conservatory of Music

The San Francisco Conservatory of Music has trained gifted young students for careers as professional musicians for seven decades. Although primarily known for its collegiate programs, the Conservatory also offers a wide variety of music classes for both children and adults.

There are free or low-cost recitals, lectures and concerts nearly every day or night of the week. Listen to voice recitals, flute and piano recitals, chamber artists, solo and ensemble performances and special events. The school is located at 1201 Ortega Street at 19th Avenue.

Call The Conservatory of Music's 24-Hour Music Line, 759-3477, for current performance schedule tape. To receive class information call 564-8086.

Stern Grove Festival

This summer, prepare a picnic and take in the sights and musical sounds of the San Francisco Midsummer Music Festival at Stern Grove. In 1938, Recreation & Park President Rosalie Stern donated this land to The City in honor of her husband Sigmund, a distinguished business and civic leader. Since 1938, the festival has played host to nearly 8,000,000 concert-goers and 25,000 performing musicians.

Call The Stern Grove Festival Association at 252-6252 to receive a season schedule. Included are dates of *Talks at the Trocadero Clubhouse,* pre-concert events at the historic Trocadero. The weekend schedule runs from June through late August. This year's fun schedule includes opera, Caribbean and Latin jazz, Mozart, English comedy, ballet, musical drama and The Duke Ellington Orchestra. Special membership packages are available, too. Great weekend event in a beautiful eucalyptus grove setting! Located at 19th Avenue & Wawona, at Sloat Blvd.

Old St. Mary's Concerts

Voice, quintet, piano and organ recitals are held Tuesdays at noon at Old St. Mary's Church at California and Grant in Chinatown. Call 986-4388 for scheduled events.

The Women's Philharmonic

Celebrating 10 years, this dynamic orchestra brings you exciting composers, accomplished performers and dazzling innovators such as the San Francisco Girls' Chorus. For concert and membership information, call 543-2297. Volunteers are also needed to help with the monthly musical program.

Epicenter Zone

475 Valencia Street (Second Floor)
431-2725
Wed.-Fri. 3 p.m. - 8 p.m.
Sat. Noon -7 p.m.
Sun. 1 p.m. - 7 p.m.

Epicenter Zone is an all-volunteer used-record/tape/CD shop that stocks punk, hardcore, industrial and garage noise rock-'n'-roll, etc. Community meetings are held the first and third Sunday of the month at 6:30 p.m.

Festivals, Street Fairs and Much More...

The Visitor Information Center offers a **24-Hour Events Hotline** for information and schedules of events citywide. Call 391-2001 to find out about street fairs, music and dance, cultural events, special ceremonies and more.

Blue Bear
School of
American Music

The Blue Bear School of American Music at Fort Mason Center, Building D, teaches rock-'n'-roll, R&B and other American musical forms. Many know it as the place where star Huey Lewis (of Huey Lewis and the News) learned his chops. Call 673-3600 for the free catalog of classes. There is an Oakland school, too.

Audium: Sound Idea!

"Sound sculptured space" is the way Stan Shaff describes his Audium, a 49-seat sound theatre that surrounds the listener top, bottom and sides with 136 loudspeakers. This relatively "underground" sound fest has been in process for nearly 25 years.

Every Friday and Saturday night at 8:30 p.m. the aural circus begins, a panjandrum of leaping tubas, rusting leaves and choir-like other-world music, manipulated noise and sound.

The carefully designed and endlessly tested sound-stage is located at 1616 Bush Street, a converted doughnut shop. Shaff, a semi-retired teacher, began the Audium experiment with a partner years ago. After receiving a Federal grant, he recently moved the event into its current location.

The concert is analog (not computerized) and Shaff himself operates a cockpit of sound equipment and sound sources that rivals The Wizard of Oz at work behind his Emerald Palace curtain. "I found that space itself is an element in sound—like a harmony or melody—and exploring that has been our pleasure."

Call 771-1616 for information. Tickets are $8.00 at the door, but call ahead.

San Francisco's Intimate Theatres

By Jean Schiffman, Editor *Callboard* **Magazine**

If you dare to venture into the out-of-the-way corners of The City—to poke around in the quaint alleys of North Beach, ride an elevator to the top floor of a Financial District skyscraper after dark or take the 30 Stockton through Chinatown to fog-shrouded Fort Mason—you can find theatre in the most unusual places in San Francisco.

Since the Gold Rush, SF has been a theatre town. With its climate, beautiful scenery and diverse ethnicity, it has served as a magnet for artists, writers and musicians of all types.

Within the city limits alone you have your choice of approximately 85 theatres, ranging from the giant **American Conservatory Theater** downtown, with its rotating repertory, to the tiniest of offbeat performing ensembles with no fixed address, such as the **Z Collective.** Sometimes the tiny ones, fresh talent experimenting with new material—no fixed lease and nothing much to lose—are the most intriguing. The tickets are cheap, too, and jeans and T-shirts are the usual dress code.

Take **Thick Description**. This tiny troupe of multiracial actors tackles the classics (last season a Greek tragedy) as well as the most avante-garde of American playwrights (Peter Mattei's absurdist *Tiny Dimes* was a recent production, as was a new take-off on *Ben-Hur*). Their venues range from the Mission Cultural Center in the heart of the Mission to small spaces in trendy South-of-Market locations. **Thick Description** could pop up anywhere.

Then there's the **Z Collective.** They were originally a group of waiters at a popular yuppie restaurant who banded together to perform. Their *Goodnight Desdemona*, a send-up of Shakespeare, proved their comedic skills are on par with theater companies five times their size. They use ingenuity when staging shows, recently placing an office-intrigue comedy in a downtown office building.

The Actor's Theatre makes clever use of a postage-stamp-size stage on the upper level of a downtown building. Organized by students at one of The City's most popular acting schools, this group always manages to offer West Coast and Bay Area premieres of shows that have triumphed in New York.

Let's not skip a group that has become a San Francisco fixture, **A Traveling Jewish Theatre**. The troupe consists of two men and a woman who have written and performed as a tight ensemble for decades. They create performance pieces, often based on such ancient Jewish legends as the Dybbuk. It may be hard to catch them in town, as they travel all over the world, but the bonus is that while they're here you can see works-in-progress and watch a piece develop.

At the cavernous **On Broadway Theatre** in North Beach, you can check out a number of small theatre companies (and sip a cappuccino afterward at one of many cafes).

On the other side of town, in the Tenderloin, **EXITheatre** produces a variety of material, including plays of social relevance, as befits a theatre company based in an inner-city setting. They keep ticket prices low so that the local community can afford to come. They also occasionally open their doors for a free neighborhood performance.

For never-before-seen-by-human-eyes theatre, check out **Brava For Women in the Arts.** This organization gives women a chance to try out new material, often for the first time, in a low-tech, low-cost setting. Frequently it's a solo show. Venues change, but you'll find **Brava** in the Mission.

The Marsh ("a breeding ground for new work") showcases new work by cutting-edge performers and writers. The difference is that The Marsh is actually a location as well as a presenter, housed in the very tiny Cafe

Poet Under Saturn

Bravo! We were pleased with this one-man performance written and performed by Phil Lumsden and directed by Julie Herrod at EXITheatre this past January. We are allowed into the one-room apartment of 19th-Century French poet and writer Paul Verlaine. The one-hour monologue centers on the poet's rocky past and philosophy. It powerfully conveys the hallucinogenic qualities of absinthe, a bitter green liqueur made from wormwood and herbs. Phil's performance was fun and allowed for rompous delight amidst a tale of poetic decadence and human darkness.

Director Julie Herrod did a great job directing the intimate work, highlighting poet Verlaine's gleeful impishness. Julie, by the way, played the little girl Gloria in the 1967 classic film *Wait Until Dark,* starring Audrey Hepburn and Alan Arkin! We'll look forward to Phil and Julie's next work...

Beano in the Mission. You can buy an espresso before the show in the adjoining cafe. (Also reassuring, there's a nearby parking lot.) The schedule is dizzying: there's the Monday Night Marsh, the Midnight Marsh and lots of in-between Marshes where you can see the finest new talent in the Bay Area.

You can't really call them a theatre, but **Fratelli Bologna** is a much-loved gang of new vaudevillians—four very funny men—who ply their trade every Christmas with their wacky *A Bologna Christmas*. Just as you can't get through the Holidays without **ACT's** *A Christmas Carol* and the **SF Ballet's** *The Nutcracker,* you won't want to miss out on the Bolognas impersonating the nutty Weber family.

Everyone's heard of the **Pickle Family Circus**, but what about **Make-A-Circus?** This is a smaller and free version of the outdoors-in-the-park summer treat for children and adults. After the show, kids can learn to juggle or tumble from the performing clowns.

If avante-garde, high-tech multimedia inventiveness and new music is your cup of tea, you won't want to miss **Soon 3's** occasional performances, usually performed in large spaces they've transformed into a total environmental experience.

Tale Spinners' speciality is oral histories—they do wonderful things with true stories about real people, adapted by local playwrights.

Bay Area Theatresports (BATS) has converted improvisation into a competitive sporting-type event held on Monday nights. The audience really gets into this one, with referees keeping the peace.

That's only the tip of SF's intimate theatre iceberg. There are a whole host of groups that flit about The City, landing here and there for a one-nighter or a two-weekend run of something new, or something tried and true.

So how do you find out about all these groups and keep track of their erratic schedules and performance sites?

One idea is look under the heading "Theater Bay Area" in the "Pink Section" of the Sunday *Examiner & Chronicle*. Another possibility is Theater Bay Area (TBA). This nonprofit resource and communication center is the hub of theatre activity in the nine-county Bay Area.

So to really be in the know, visit or call TBA's downtown office (657 Mission) and receive a free copy of the "Hot Tickets" map that will show you where these theatres are located and will give you their box-office phone numbers. Have your name placed on the "Hot Tickets" mailing list to receive announcements of many of the shows, or read *Callboard* or the Pink Section for more.

Whether it's Latino theatre, avant-garde adventurism, the classics, circus, multimedia, solo and improvisation or kitchen sink realism—whatever your taste—there's a San Francisco intimate theatre to stir your imagination. Call Theater Bay Area at 957-1557 for information.

Jean Schiffman is Editor of Callboard, *the bible of local actors and theater artists, which lists shows, auditions, job calls, tips and career hints for the theatre worker.* Callboard *is available at Dramabooks, The Booksmith (see* Magazine Racks of SF*) and other magazine shops in the Bay Area.* THE ALMANAC *would also like to thank Liza Zenni, Director of TBA, for her fine assistance.*

Costume Closets

Next time you are looking for a certain costume for Halloween or a Masquerade Ball, don't forget your local playhouses. Many will rent you costumes from previous shows at very affordable rates. Theatre Bay Area will send you a list of SF's little theatres. Call 957-1557.

The Children's Drama Service

This traveling troupe of NCJW players and stagehands delivers theatre shows such as *Cinderella* to Bay Area disabled children. If you'd like to contribute your singing, dancing or acting talents, call Esther Kalins at 434-2688.

The San Francisco Mime Troupe— Theatre in the Parks

Each summer since 1959, the SF Mime Troupe has entertained thousands of San Franciscans with their classic comedia dell'arte-style performances. The shows are free and take place in many of SF's smaller parks, with the season opener often held on the Fourth of July in Dolores Park.

The extremely popular summer shows daringly spoof current social and political topics, including war and foreign intervention, Israeli-Palestinian conflict, abortion and freedom of choice and a host of current world dilemmas.

The multi-cultural cast helps us remember that no matter how bad it gets, there's always room for laughter. Families, dogs and even the Troupe band commingle in one of The City's most well-known summer theatre offerings. This summer, don't miss the sun, the grass, the theatre and the fun!

This group recently won a Tony Award for their work. Contrary to the title, they are not a mime troupe, but rather offer fresh, original plays that they write and produce themselves. To find out more, look for their schedule in the "Pink Section," or call 285-1720 for performance information.

Harlequin and Columbine bid you adieu . . .

For an excellent summary of San Francisco's colorful stage history, purchase *The San Francisco Stage: From Gold Rush to Golden Spike* and *The SF Stage: From Golden Spike to Great Earthquake*, two comprehensive and entertaining titles written by Misha Berson, Bay Area theatre expert and writer. Both titles are available at The SF Performing Arts Library and at other booksellers. (See *Little Libraries* for SF PALM.) Just $15.00/title.

Almanac Green

Friends of the Urban Forest

Friends of the Urban Forest (FUF) is a SF non-profit organization committed to the belief that trees are vital to a livable urban environment. If your neighborhood lacks trees, these folks can help you and your friends and neighbors to plant your block. The FUF staff will match funds, provide you with necessary city permits and help you gain the cooperation of your neighbors. They can help provide trees at low cost, lend you the special tools you'll need and offer professional consulting.

This carefully considered program has helped to plant and maintain over 10,000 trees since its inception in 1981. Schools and businesses are encouraged to get involved. Call FUF at 543-5000. Ask them to send you information on how to get started in helping to "grow" The City into the 21st Century.

Treescapes: **FUF Journal**

Your membership in FUF brings you *Treescapes*, the organization's bright, informative newsletter, chock-full of articles and tips on trees and tree care. *Treescapes* recently reported that over 3,400 City trees died from last December's freeze and the drought. FUF is making sure that these trees are replaced, not removed and cemented over. When the young East Bay ReLeaf group becomes part of FUF in late 1992, FUF will be helping to repair the devastation caused by the great Oakland Hills fire, too. *Treescapes* documents the group's achievements and teaches about trees. It is just one more rewarding reason to become a member of FUF and show your support for a green San Francisco.

Tree Care for Homeowners

by James E. Biller, American Society of Consulting Arborists

Since beautification begins with removing ugliness, let's begin tree care by avoiding improper tree work that causes ugliness. Using pole-climbing spikes on trees might head the list. Outlawed in many states, pole-spikes on a live tree should immediately alert us to a tree climber who has either no tree care education or no regard for our trees. This person should be summarily invited to leave our property.

Next, after making sure we haven't hired a "butcher" instead of an arborist, let's understand a few things about trees. If we realize that some yard trees are destined to get too big in time, we can, in good conscience, remove them when they're still small enough to put in a trash can. (A call to your local State Extension office will secure a list of undesirable trees.) If this is done regularly, you will not have to deal with many problems later on, such as tent caterpillars, dutch elm diseases, fire, heartwood rot and others.

After getting rid of unwelcome attempts by Mother Nature to landscape our property, let's turn our attention to mature tree care. Experts now agree that trees should not have radical crown reduction, sometimes called topping, drop crotching, pollarding or "hat racking," usually recognized as a means of reducing tree size. Since this is a conspicious form of tree work, many homeowners accept it as a proper form of tree care. It's quite wrong.

If you talk to the same "expert" who did this to a neighbor's trees (and sold the neighbor a bill of goods), no doubt you will get the same expert opinion from both the neighbor and his tree man. Beware! There are far too many good reasons not to succumb to this butchery, though a look around will convince you it is still a common practice. We now understand how trees respond to "wounding" and what can and can't be done with impunity. Just as there are some bad doctors and lawyers...

Proper tree pruning requires some knowledge of tree biology. You must prune limbs and branches so that you do not injure the "collar" at the base of the limb or branch. The final pruning cut should be angled so that it begins in the crotch outside the collar and extends outward slightly beyond the bottom of the branch collar.

A proper cut is not flush with the parent stem, as was taught for years, but around the branch collar, leaving a slight bulge. Since most saws cut a straight line, and most branch collars would be best cut with a curving line, a compromise is called for. The cut should be made that leaves too much stub rather than cutting through the branch collar.

(It goes without saying that the weight of the limb being removed should be supported by hand or some rope rigging or the branch will tear at the bottom, causing a problem. The usual way to prevent this is to undercut the limb first a foot or so out from the parent stem and take the limb off, thus relieving the weight of the limb before making the final stem cut. A diagram of this method, called the 1-2-3 method of limb removal, is shown.)

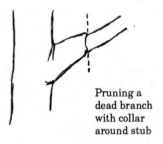

Pruning a dead branch with collar around stub

This is the first of a series of annual articles on tree care. The author, the Editor's father, owns Forman & Biller Tree Expert Company, which has served the Washington DC area since 1919. His father founded the renowned company, which has contributed to restoration and care of the grounds of many historic institutions in the DC area.

Next year's article will cover when and what to prune and the benefits of pruning...

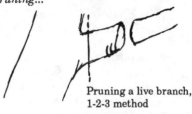

Pruning a live branch, 1-2-3 method

Tree Care Referrals

If you are looking for a tree expert in the Bay Area, for an expert opinion or work on either street trees or yard trees, the Friends of the Urban Forest suggests that you talk to these folks. The Editor cautions against blindly choosing an arborist from the phone book, and suggests that you *never* hire anyone who solicits your work off the street...

Green Dragon Gardening
Joe and Kathy Tang (SF)
(415) 751-5255

Peter Gradjansky (East Bay)
(510) 549-0955

**Western Chapter
Int'l Society of Arboriculture**
(707) 224-0736

To learn about A.S.C.A. members in your area, call John T. Duke, Exec. Dir. A.S.C.A., (303)466-2722.

Pinelli's Flowerland

Pinelli's is a quality example of the San Francisco full-service neighborhood florist. This friendly little shop has served the Bay Area's wedding, shower and special-occasion floral needs since 1927. They offer a wide assortment of ever-popular roses, irises, tulips and more. Prompt delivery and special event service are available 365 days a year (throughout the central Bay Area). They create affordable floral creations for weddings, funerals and special gifts. Credit card telephone orders on most bank cards and convenient late hours: open 9 a.m. until 8 p.m. Monday-Saturday and until 6 p.m. Sundays and Holidays. Their back-room-crafted floral designs are lovely, practical and moderately priced.

The current owners, John and Margaret Sellai, bought the shop from Mr. Pinelli and have continued the quality tradition (John was an original Pinelli's employee) for these past thirty years. The snazzy Art Deco woodcut logo embossed on their flower boxes dates from 1929.

California is home to three of the five major floral trade centers in the US, which include San Diego, Los Angeles, SF, Portland and Seattle. The City is a popular stop for the flower vendors who bring the field and hothouse-grown flowers fresh from the rich Central Valley and the lush Pacific Coast. California-grown flowers arrive fresh at Pinelli's Flowerland every day.

Raymond Clary
1915–1992:
Real San Franciscan

San Francisco lost one of its finest citizens on January 9, 1992: Raymond H. Clary. Mr. Clary was Golden Gate Park's citizen advocate these past fifty years, seeing that callous politicians did not turn the esteemed urban park into the Disneyland of San Francisco. From his early days as an Ohio soldier in The Presidio, through his years as a skilled watch-maker, historian, writer, activist and devoted husband, Mr. Clary set an example for all of us to live by in his life and his work. He will be remembered by those he touched, and missed by those who knew him well. Mr. Clary, a wise pragmatist, would have been first to admit that when he was gone there would be no other. Golden Gate Park and San Francisco simply got lucky these past fifty years...

Francis Scott Key Monument

Raymond Clary told us this story:

Mr. Clary found one of The Park's oldest and prettiest monuments, for Francis Scott Key, rotting in the gardener's yard. After months of letter writing, phone calls to City Hall and numerous petition signings, the lovely monument was restored to its present position, east of the Music Concord.

A public re-dedication ceremony was held. The workers and Mr. Clary's friends watched the final lowering of the statue. "What about a time capsule?" one worker asked, volunteering his lunchbox. They included a copy of Mr. Clary's first book (14 years in the writing) *The Making of Golden Gate Park: The Early Years 1865–1906,* a relic photograph and schedule from the 1894 Mid-Winter Fair and that morning's *San Francisco Chronicle.* The items were placed in the base beneath the fully-renewed creation.

The restoration of the Francis Scott Key statue was perhaps Raymond's fondest Park achievement out of hundreds. Although many public figures attended the day's event, (it happened to be lunch-time) not a single politician witnessed the sincere private ceremony. "Good thing," said Raymond, "They would have made a big fuss, anyway."

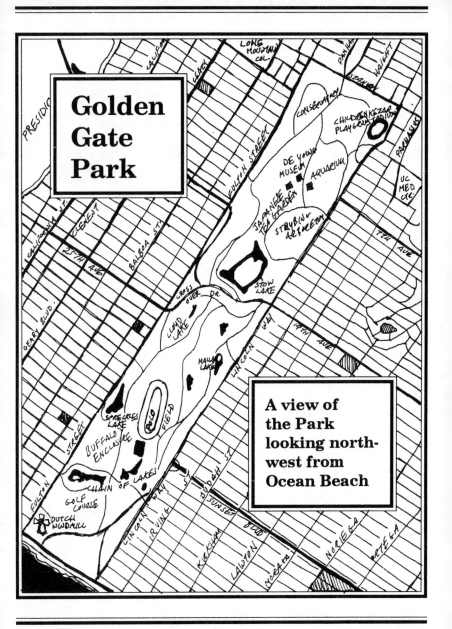

Golden Gate Park

A view of the Park looking north-west from Ocean Beach

Strybing Arboretum

Golden Gate Park
(near 9th Avenue & Lincoln Way)
Weekdays 8 a.m. - 4:30 p.m.
Weekends & Holidays 10 a.m. - 5 p.m.
Docent tours are held daily at 1:30 p.m.
The tours are free and very, very good.

The Strybing Arboretum & Botanical Gardens is one of San Francisco's finest treasures. San Francisco and Northern California have a Mediterranean climate, one of five regions in the world that do. (They generally occur on the south/west coasts of continents). Strybing Arboretum gardens showcase the plants, flowers, grasses and trees that dwell in these special coastal environments.

Strybing is also home to The Strybing Arboretum Society and The Helen Crocker Russell Library. The Society advances the splendor of the gardens and encourages learning and teaching; the library houses over 14,000 books and videos and carries over 300 wildlife and horticulture periodicals. The library is open to the public daily from 10 a.m. to 4 p.m. (The Strybing Bookstore is a great resource, too.)

Gardens at The Arboretum include Eastern and Southwestern Australia, New Zealand, South America, Asia and, of course, California. The gardens are quiet, contemplative places for walking and wandering, with trails leading through the several dozen featured gardens. Leave your Walkman at home. Several hundred varieties of birds call Strybing home at one time or another through the seasons. Their chatter and music helps ease city tensions, as do the well-planned gardens and the sweet, wet air of The Strybing Arboretum.

This year Strybing is looking great after a very wet spring. Damage done by last year's unusually cold winter has largely been replaced by blooming growth and blossoming flowers.

Strybing holds Northern California's largest greenhouse sale each Spring and many smaller sales and shows of all kinds throughout the year. Call Strybing Arboretum for details at 661-1316. Membership in The Strybing Arboretum Society will keep you up-to-date on a myriad of "green" opportunities for San Franciscans.

The Garden for the Environment is located at the corner of Seventh Avenue and Lawton near Laguna Honda. In just a few short years, the rubble-filled lot has been transformed into a lovely demonstration garden for San Franciscans to learn from and enjoy. The Water Dept., SLUG (SF League of Urban Gardeners), the SF Recycling Program and many private businesses joined to build the garden. It features drought-tolerant plants, vegetable beds in a "low tech/high growth" greenhouse and a home composting learning center. Visit soon.

BayKeeper volunteers patrol our Bay Area waters, searching for pollution and poachers. They include 300 kayakers, fishermen and aircraft pilots, who call a toll-free hotline (1-800-KEEP-BAY) to report suspicious activities or environmental dangers. If you witness dumping, poaching or similiar acts of environmental vandalism in The Bay, you can call these tireless guardians of the Bay's water and wildlife. Their office is located at Fort Mason Center (567-4401).

Non-Toxic Home Pest Control

A recently published book entitled *Tiny Game Hunting* offers environmentally healthy ways to trap and kill pests in your home or garden. Written by Hilary Klein and Adrian Wenner of Santa Barbara, the book is a valuable home reference and is available for just $8.50 at Builder's Booksource and other book shops. This practical book details each particular problem and offers low-cost and effective non-toxic techniques. Recommended home resource for San Franciscans living in older buildings. (See *Magazines & Booksellers of San Francisco* for Builder's Booksource.)

FUF Walking Tours

Join FUF for their fantastic City guided tour series, featured in this ALMANAC under *Day Trips*. Call 543-5000 for Spring–Fall tour brochure. FUF has a fine membership program, too, which will keep you updated on plantings and teach you a great deal about our trees. They offer a low-cost student kit, allowing teachers to impart all this green knowledge in their classrooms, too.

SCRAP

SCRAP answers a question that THE ALMANAC has been asking for two years, what to do with seemingly useful items such as accumulated Häagen-Dazs tops!

SCRAP (Scrounger's Center for Reuseable Art Parts) recently received a $15,000 grant from San Francisco's Recycling Program. The SF School District offered the group a space at Sunshine School at 2730 Bryant Street, where they collect clean milk cartons, telephone wire, office items, spools, reusable paper products, plastic tops and bottles, egg cartons, twist ties and more, to be distributed to school art programs.

SCRAP encourages individual dropoffs when open Tuesdays and Thursdays and can pick up materials from businesses that offer by-products. Call 647-1746. There is a drop-box just inside the door of the school to save you the trip up to SCRAP on the second floor, open school days. Do drop in; see for yourself the colorful collection of day-to-day "stuff."

80 Community Gardens

"Oh, I'd better hurry. I've got to get some seeds. I've got to get some seeds, right away. Nothing's planted. I don't have a thing in the ground."
—Willy Loman, *Death of a Salesman* by Arthur Miller

Community gardens give yardless apartment dwellers a chance to stake out a little patch of vegetables or flowers all their own. SLUG (San Francisco League of Urban Gardeners) offers a complete listing of 80 City public gardens. Call 469-0110 for the list of gardens and contact persons.

The Ecology Center Store

The Ecology Center in Berkeley offers hundreds of books, magazines and newsletters on recycling, ecology and conservation. The ecological living section sells rechargeable batteries, non-toxic paint and organic gardening supplies. Their newsletter, *Ecology Center Terrain,* is a valuable resource. The Ecology Center Library is open at all times to the public for research. The library maintains a media clipping service that offers files in hundreds of categories. Call 548-2220 for information, for membership or to volunteer time or resources. Visit soon. Located at 2530 San Pablo Avenue, several blocks east of University Avenue.

Restoring the Bay Campaign

In the San Francisco Bay, a part of the San Francisco Bay-Delta Estuary, 16 California rivers meet the salt water of the Pacific Ocean. The meeting and mixing of fresh and salt water, and the Bay's rare Mediterranean climate, provide a setting for a highly diverse community of plants and animals.

Bay Area growth has brought great losses to the Bay. Today, only 550 of the original 780 sq. miles of the Bay remain unclaimed by coastal filling; 90–95% of the Bay's tidal wetlands have been destroyed since 1899. In addition, six oil refineries and dozens of municipal and commercial waste operations contribute to pollution of Bay water. Construction of Bay-front buildings, dredging, complexes and freeways further limit and pollute natural habitats for plants, fish and San Francisco Bay Area wildlife.

The Restoring the Bay Campaign has developed a comprehensive action plan to this end. A project of The Save San Francisco Bay Association, the activities of thirty environmental groups are coordinated to:

1) protect fish and wildlife;
2) restore wetlands and creeks;
3) develop an environmentally sound dredging and dredge disposal program;
4) improve water quality by removing toxins;
5) secure adequate fresh water to the Bay from the Delta;
6) promote sensitive land use and transportation;
7) promote ecological park planning;
8) educate and involve all citizens in restoration of the Bay.

Whether you want to don rubber waders and gloves and give a stretch of Bay shoreline a little TLC, telephone fellow environmentalists and legislators or do computer graphics or staff work, The Restoring the Bay Campaign can use your help in many creative ways. You can help protect and restore the Bay by speaking to groups or by doing field and wetland restoration projects, research photography, leading shoreline walks, writing monthly letters or helping with media/PR projects.

Call (510) 452-9261 to receive *The Citizens' Agenda,* which outlines the Bay program. Help restore the San Francisco Bay we love to call home!

Local Farmers' Markets

Heart of the City Farmers' Market

Wed., Sun. 7 a.m. - 5 p.m.
United Nations Plaza, Market & Hyde
(near Main Library)
For information call 558-9455

Alemany Farmers' Market

Tues.-Sat. 5 a.m. - 5 p.m.
Alemany Blvd. & I-280 (by 101 Split)
For information call 647-9423

The Ecology Center Farmers' Market (Berkeley)

Tues. 1 p.m. - Dusk
Derby Street (at Milvia)
Sat. 10 a.m. - 2 p.m.
Center Street (at Milvia)
For information call (510) 548-2220

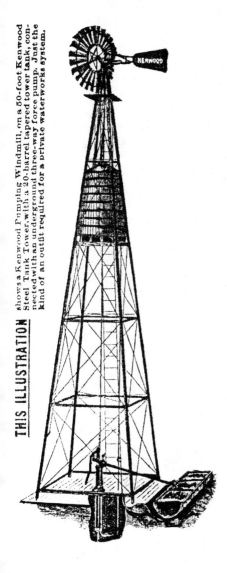

THIS ILLUSTRATION shows a Kenwood Pumping Windmill, on a 50-foot Kenwood Steel Tank Tower, with a 20-barrel tapered tower tank, connected with an underground three-way force pump. Just the kind of an outfit required for a private waterworks system.

Water Wells in The City

In 1912–13 respected City Engineer M.M. O'Shaugnessy did a very smart thing. He mapped the location of the existing water-wells throughout San Francisco. As Hetch Hetchy was being built (today's modern City water supply), such a map might one day be valuable. His crew surveyed 900 of the active wells around town, testing them for taste (potability), flow (gallons per hour) and temperature.

The engineer chronicled that Stanyan Street clearly traced The City's natural watershed. All ground water east of Stanyan flowed to the Bay. All the spring-water west of Stanyan found its way to the Pacific. He noted that there was no shortage of ground water under The City, and that in times of drought the springs did not decrease one iota in their output of cold, clean water. He even noted that one of the largest stands of fresh-water, out of thousands of plugged or existing wells, was under Ocean Beach. Lurking only a hundred feet *beneath* the salt water was a vast fresh-water supply!

Of course, the water hasn't gone anywhere. To this day there's enough ground water to irrigate all the parks, clean the streets, cool our machinery and provide emergency wells/pumps for firefighting. We're going to re-publish this mapbook soon. Send us a postcard if you're interested...

SF/SPCA & Pet Care

The San Francisco Society for the Prevention of Cruelty to Animals (SF/SPCA) is one of America's most successful animal welfare organizations. The Animal Care Center at 2500 16th Street provides refuge, nourishment, medical care, adoption services and love to homeless animals.

April 18, 1993 marks the 125th Anniversary of the SF/SPCA. Petwalk '93 will be held May 8th in Sharon Meadow and the Great SF/SPCA Cat and Dog Fair is scheduled for Fort Mason in Fall 1993. Call 554-3000 for details.

If you love animals and want to help, the SPCA offers a broad-based volunteer program. You can become an adoption counselor, outreach volunteer, dog walker or helper for one of many special projects. To volunteer call 554-3000 and ask to speak to the Volunteer Coordinator. There are other ways to help the animals, too, including SF/SPCA membership and foster care for animals too young to be adopted.

Human Kindness: Two unaltered cats and their offspring can parent more than 150,000 kittens within seven years! Each year, 13 million cats and dogs are euthanized in the United States alone. Millions more who live abandoned and wild become victims of disease, accidents, poisoning and predators.

Get your dog or cat spayed or neutered. Most reasons for not doing so are plain foolishness.

Dog Outings: The SF Recreation & Park Department prints a handy brochure that clearly indicates park areas where dogs may legally romp unharnessed. Pick up a brochure at McLaren Lodge, Oak and Stanyan.

Poodle Pride: The SPCA offers a grooming school for pets and pet groomers. Call 554-3000 for details.

SPCA and the Cable Cars

Many don't know it, but the SF/SPCA had a hand in the establishment of SF's premier ambassadors, the cable cars! Andrew Halladie, cable car inventor and advocate, was mocked by many in his day.

One of his driving reasons for creating the cable car system was to save men and horses from the terrible horse-cart accidents that were frequent on SF's steep hills. The SPCA appreciated Halladie's efforts and campaigned vocally for acceptance of his ideas by the public and political leaders. A powerful and successful organization even in those early days, they helped Halladie see his dream come true.

Adopt a Pet: If you want to adopt a pet, the SF/SPCA will handle all of the grateful dog or cat's tests, early care and more. There is a one-time adoption fee of $28.00 per animal (plus tax), which includes spay/neuter services.

Cold at night? Bored at breakfast? Maybe a pet adopted from the SF/SPCA is just what the doctor ordered. Call the SF/SPCA at 554-3000 for information. The office is open Monday - Saturday 11 a.m. - 4 p.m.

Spay/Neuter Clinic

The SF/SPCA offers an inexpensive pet Spay/Neuter Clinic. Male dogs cost $25.00 to neuter, female pooches $35.00 to spay. Male cats are $20.00, female cats are $25.00. You must have your pet fully vaccinated first, or show proof of your animal's DHLPP/FVRCP series. The SF/SPCA advises you to pick up a copy of the SPCA pamphlet *Information About Your Pet's Appointment* before making final plans and reserving spay/neuter services. Call 554-3000.

The SF/SPCA Humane Education Program

Article by Richard Avanzino
President SF/SPCA

The San Francisco
SPCA

The little five-year-old girl shrieked in horror when she was told that the SPCA was bringing a dog to her after-school class at the youth center. Her mother had told her that dogs were dangerous and that she should stay away from them. She begged the teachers to let her leave the room. After some discussion, the teachers decided to have the little girl sit in an adjoining room with an accompanying teacher and watch through an opening in the partition.

As she peered through the peephole, an affable golden retriever ambled into the classroom. The girl watched the dog; it certainly didn't look scary. She crept back into the room, adult companion in tow, and sat a comfortable distance from the soft orange canine. As the woman who brought the dog talked about proper pet care, the girl stared at the serene animal in amazement. And when it came time for the kids to pet the dog, she took a turn. In fact, she liked it so much she went back for "seconds."

Not every child is so profoundly touched by the San Francisco SPCA's Humane Education Program, but we hope each

walks away with a greater respect for animals. The program's classroom visits are designed to help each child become more appreciative of the Earth's creatures and environmental concerns. By visiting classrooms, providing contact with animals and making a wide array of educational materials available, the SF/SPCA seeks to instill in students a heightened awareness of all living things.

SF/SPCA staff and volunteers, along with dogs, guinea pigs, rabbits, hamsters, lizards, snakes and other animal educators, visit classrooms to discuss pet care, endangered species, pet over-population and other topics about animals and the environment. Students are encouraged to discuss their thoughts and feelings about animals, ask questions and, in most cases, touch the visiting animal.

To further promote an appreciation of animals and the role they play in our environment, the SF/SPCA has made a comprehensive humane education curriculum available to California's elementary school teachers. The guide deals with such topics as California wildlife, petcare and animal-related careers. The materials also focus on the physical characteristics of animals, how they communicate and what they need to live.

Students also have an opportunity to take field trips to the SF/SPCA Education Resource Center, where they can meet both pets and non-releasable wild animals. The animals serve as a focal point for discussion of the animal world's complexities and the respect and care animals need and deserve.

All of the above services and materials are provided free of charge to more than 800 educators and 24,000 students in San Francisco, thanks to the generosity of friends and members of the San Francisco SPCA.

Thanks to Richard Avanzino, President of the SF/SPCA, for his unceasing efforts on behalf of animals in The City. To support the SF/SPCA's Humane Education efforts, or to request more information, write to The San Francisco SPCA, Humane Education Program, 2500 16th Street, SF, CA 94103, or call (415) 554-3000.

Our Animals

SF/SPCA supporters receive the award-winning publication, *Our Animals.* Chock-full of informative articles about all kinds of pets, *Our Animals* is just one more great reason to become a SF/SPCA member. Call 554-3000 to receive a membership packet. Tell them Kid Gloves, the ALMANAC Editor-Cat, sent you!

ALMANAC Editor-Cat Kid Gloves

These are some of our favorite veterinarians...

Here are some local vets we can heartily recommend; they are favorites with family, friends and pets. Friendly Park Animal Hospital happens to be the veterinarian of manx-tailed ALMANAC Editor-Cat Kid Gloves!

All offer a complete range of animal services, most compassionate staffs and highly skilled DVM's. (All offer emergency care.) Call for information.

Park Animal Hospital
1207 Ninth Avenue
(at Lincoln Way)
753-8485
Easy free parking

Marina Pet Hospital
2024 Lombard
(btwn. Fillmore & Webster)
921-0410
Convenient public parking

Ocean Avenue Veterinary Hospital
1001 Ocean Avenue
(across from City College)
587-5327

Mission Pet Hospital
720 Valencia (at 18th St.)
552-1969
(service until 10 p.m., except Saturdays)

In Memoriam . . .

Elizabeth, the ALMANAC artist, lost her beloved cat Mocha to illness on June 13th of this year. Mocha was found searching through garbage cans by an SF/SPCA volunteer in 1986. She was very skinny and just about ready to give birth to a litter of kittens. She was taken in to SPCA-sponsored foster care until she had her litter and homes could be found for all her offspring. Shortly thereafter, someone left two kittens, who couldn't have been more than 14-days-old, on the SF/SPCA steps. Amazingly, Mocha adopted them right away! Elizabeth was loath to break up this intrepid family, and so she adopted all three of them!

At first, Mocha was very wary of people, but soon she became extremely affectionate, especially toward anyone wearing denim! She is missed very much by Elizabeth, Michael, Mewzette and Chloe. Thanks to everyone at the SF/SPCA for giving these guys a second chance.

THE SAN FRANCISCO ALMANAC offers a profitable sales plan for
non-profits and fundraising groups in The City.
For information about how your members can
purchase ALMANACS to help generate funds,
please contact the Editor.

Our Community: Groups & Organizations

THE ALMANAC spotlights some of the best local service organizations in San Francisco, "The City that Knows How."

California Lawyers for the Arts

When art and artists meet law and money, California Lawyers for the Arts (CUA) is there to offer an accessible alternative. The $25 membership fee provides access to a wide range of inexpensive legal and support services. The drop-in copyright clinic alone is worth the price of membership. CLA also sponsors Arthouse/SF, a live/work artists' collective/information bureau that helps artists navigate the maze of laws and challenges they face as studio owners. To contact CLA call 775-7715. To contact Arthouse/SF call 554-9679.

SCORE

Folks going into business for themselves can attend a one-day lecture with SCORE, the Service Corps of Retired Executives. Their pre-business workshops give you a chance to ask questions of accomplished business people in The City. Call 744-6827 weekdays 10 a.m. - 2 p.m. Small fee for valuable course. Recommended reality lesson for start-up businesses!

Jewish Vocational & Career Counseling Service

Since 1973, the Jewish Vocational Service (JVS) has provided employers with the largest free public listing service in San Francisco. As a non-profit, non-sectarian agency, JVS charges no fee to employers for candidate screening, referral or placement. Call JVS at 391-3600 next time you have a job opening. Their office has moved to larger quarters at 77 Geary Street.

The Housing Committee at Old St. Mary's Church

Did you know that two-thirds of San Franciscans rent? The Housing Committee at Old St. Mary's is an invaluable organization for any San Franciscan having landlord/tenant problems. They offer telephone counseling, direct assistance, workshops, a landlord/tenant legal library and much more. The group began in 1979 and has grown from seven original volunteers to include hundreds of members. If you'd like to receive assistance, offer resources or volunteer, call the Housing Committee at 398-0724. Their informative membership publication, *The Renter's Voice*, is included with your membership benefits.

The Women's Building

The Women's Building is a central clearinghouse for information and services, providing thousands of women throughout the Bay Area with the assistance they need. It has been home to more than 125 important new projects in the past decade.

The building houses organizations that provide a range of resources to women. A primary goal is addressing the needs of women most marginalized in our society: women of color, low-income women and lesbians.

Programs within the building include *La Casa de Las Madres,* a shelter for battered women and their families; a *Women's HIV Support Center; San Francisco Women Against Rape; OPTIONS for Women Over Forty; The Women's Cancer Research Center; Harvey Milk Democratic Club; Lesbian Agenda for Action; The Women's Foundation; NOW; Alice B. Toklas Democratic Club; Maestros por la Paz (Teachers For Peace); The Bay Area Women's Philharmonic Orchestra* and more. Special events are held in the building's auditorium on a regular basis, including numerous fundraisers for the various groups.

If you can help, your membership will assist many. Hundreds of women each month call or visit the building seeking job referrals, housing information and other resources.

A Tenth Anniversary Campaign has begun, with the goal of raising $1.8 million. This money will finish paying for the building at 3543 18th Street, will allow renovation to be completed and will expedite upgrading and expanding available office space.

Women's Building Holiday Arts & Crafts Fair

One fund-raising effort that has gained attention over the past ten years is The Women's Building Arts and Crafts Fair, held before Christmas each year at Fort Mason Center. The holiday shopping, cooking and multicultural entertainment make for several weekends of enjoyment and giving. These holiday gifts bear doubly good tidings.

Call The Women's Building in late November for Crafts Fair details. Volunteers are always required for this event, and word is it's really fun! (You get a great T-shirt, too. One four-hour shift requested.) If you are interested in contributing to The Women's Building's vital programs, call 431-1180 and ask for the Volunteer Coordinator.

SF Jewish Community Center

Membership in the SFJCC brings so many benefits that we couldn't begin to list them all. (We suggest you begin with their entertaining and educational members' catalogue.) The center offers a fitness and athletic center and pool, educational classes and mini-courses, parties, performances and more. Membership brings substantial discounts on SF Symphony tickets, Price Club membership and more.

Drop by to explore, and receive a copy of the current SFJCC bi-monthly catalogue. Call The San Francisco Jewish Community Center at 346-6040, or visit their office at 3200 California Street (at Presidio) for information about this rich network of enrichment opportunities for diverse San Franciscans.

THE ALMANAC highly recommends the delightfully informal City Cafe, too, where you can enjoy a PB & J, a Coke and some great potato salad for about $4.00. Open to the public daily.

The Junior League of San Francisco

The Junior League is an organization of women committed to promoting volunteerism, and to improving the community through the effective action of trained volunteers. Its purpose is educational and charitable; it annually donates thousands of volunteer hours and proceeds to a number of Bay Area agencies. A portion of these funds are raised by The Next-to-New Shop. (see *ALMANAC White Elephant*).

The SF Junior League supports a wide range of community groups each year, including those such as:

A Safe Place
AIDS Home Care and Hospice
Bay Area Women's Resource Center
Bread & Roses
Friends of St. Francis Center
Hamilton Family Center
Hope House
La Casa de Las Madres
Purpose Project
San Francisco Educational Services
Volunteer Legal Services
Whitney High Risk Clinic
Youth Advocates/HIV Program
Youth in Arts
...and others.

Outdoors Unlimited

Outdoors Unlimited is a cooperative resource center for outdoor recreation and adventure, located on the UCSF campus at Parnassus between 3rd and 4th Aves. They provide skills training, gear rental, trip planning and a place to meet others with similar interests.

Camping gear, car racks, aquatic recreation and cross-country skiing equipment is available at low rates; there is a diverse quarterly offering of classes, trips and workshops. To receive the quarterly catalogue and schedule, send a legal-size SASE with 52¢ postage to: Outdoors Unlimited, Box 0234 A, University of California, SF, CA 94143. The organization is funded by membership and U of C support. Call OU at 476-2078 for volunteer/member info.

Volunteer Center

This United Way organization helps connect volunteers with opportunities that vary to fit their talents and schedules. Anyone can help; jobs include everything from part-time tutoring to graphic design to clean-up. Each December, the Volunteer Center publishes a wish-list, helping groups locate second-hand office equipment and more. Located at 1160 Battery St. #400. Call 982-8999 for volunteer information.

Hospitality House

Since 1967, the Hospitality House has served as a resource/neighborhood center at 146 Leavenworth Street. The program includes a community artist studio and classes, street outreach, employment assistance and individual and group counseling.

Hospitality House also publishes *The Tenderloin Times*, one of The City's finest newspapers. If you can offer your resources, or would like more information, call HH at 776-2102. Happy 25th Birthday, Hospitality House!

Senior Information

Senior Information, Referral and Health Promotion is an official source of information about services and resources in San Francisco for persons sixty-years and over.

In The City, this service is provided by the Department of Public Health. The office is open weekdays 8 a.m. - 5 p.m. and is located at 1182 Market Street, Room 212. Twenty-four hour telephone service is available at 626-1033.

Visual Aid

This entirely volunteer organization of artists, art dealers and art supporters is dedicated to financially supporting artists with AIDS and other life-threatening illnesses so that they can continue their work. Call 391-9663 for information.

Media Alliance

Media Alliance, located at Fort Mason Center, serves as a resource pool for people in the media. Their job listings service is extremely popular, with 25–50 new listings each month. Media Alliance offers courses on publication skills, proofreading, radio broadcasting, graphic design, grant research and more. Public forums spotlight the hot issues in media. Computer training is available, too. *Bay Area Censored* is their annual review of the hottest local stories that were either not covered or under-covered by the local media. To contact Media Alliance, call their office Mondays or Fridays 1 p.m. - 5 p.m. or Wednesdays 1 p.m. - 8 p.m., 441-2557.

Community Boards: Conflict Mediation

This free conflict resolution service offers a mediation program for neighbors, family members, spouses or partners, housemates, landlords and tenants and friends. It is open to anyone. Call 863-6100 for details. The office is at 1540 Market Street, Room 490. Programs like this work best when both sides respect the no-win prospects of many lawsuits.

SF Lawyers' Committee for Urban Affairs

This organization operates a legal clinic for lower-income individuals or families, offering legal services by some of SF's biggest law firms at low or no cost. There are a range of services; call 543-9444 weekdays 9 a.m. - 5 p.m. for Legal Clinic information and procedures.

SF Bar Association Lawyer Referral Service

The "1-800-LAWYER" service of the legal profession, the Bar offers a quality lawyer referral service. Call 764-1616 for referral. THE ALMANAC has used this resource with great results.

National Council of Jewish Women

The National Council of Jewish Women was founded in 1893. Its volunteer members are dedicated to serving the local home community, the nation and Israel through advocacy and direct services. The San Francisco Section supports numerous beneficial local programs. If you can help, contact NCJW. An active and devoted City organization, NCJW helps to support these and other programs in The City:

BARGAIN MART THRIFT SHOP

1823 Divisadero Street
(Btwn. Pine & Bush)

Hours: Monday - Saturday
10 a.m. - 4:45 p.m.
(415) 921-7380

NATIONAL COUNCIL OF JEWISH WOMEN

WICS—Women in Community Service working together to help young women help themselves in today's job market.

Bargain Mart—The popular Divisadero Street thrift shop whose profits help make San Francisco-Section NCJW services possible. Donations sought.

Menorah Mart—A non-profit Jewish grocery at a Jewish senior residence, Menorah Park.

Library Project—Adults working with children in SF school libraries.

Pathways to English—A tutorial program in conjunction with the SF School Volunteers, teaching reading and language skills to children and young adults.

Children's Drama Service—A traveling theatre group that performs for disabled children in special schools in the Bay Area (see *Theatre*).

Scholarship Program for Youth

Assistance to the Mayor's Task Force for the Homeless.

These are just some of the ways you can help as a NCJW member or volunteer. Call NCJW at 346-4600.

Apprentice Alliance

Apprentices and masters are linked through this growing organization, which provides persons who desire to learn a trade, skill or career an opportunity to get started *in the field*.

Alliance masters are businesses and well-established freelancers in many areas, including art, business and trade. Masters have the opportunity to gain the help of a serious, energetic helper while promoting themselves in over 5,000 annual directories.

Call Apprentice Alliance and order their 80-page directory for just $6.00. The service costs under $150 for masters or apprentices. Approximately 100 masters are listed. (The group is always looking for new masters, too.)

Ceramics, children's clothing, video, photography and film, museum skills, painting and printmaking, textiles, design, music and recording, piano tuning, construction, framing, landscaping, woodwork, publishing and writing...a plethora of *real life* jobs to wet your feet in the business and begin to explore career options.

Call 863-8661. Anne-Marie Theilen, Director of Apprentice Alliance, adds that she encourages inquiries from both prospective masters and apprentices, to assist in their careers.

Apprentice Alliance Fact Sheet

Since its founding in 1977, this organization has sponsored 3,458 apprentices and has worked in partnership with over 500 masters.

What is an apprenticeship?

It's job training! Apprentices acquire skills that will lead to employment. The nature of this training depends on the master and the apprentice. Some work 10–15 hours a week, others full-time, for periods of 1–3 months, 6 months or one year.

What does it cost?

For apprentices, $25 a year. For masters, $50 a year. After a trial period, both the apprentice and the master must pay a placement fee of $100.

How do I find out more?

The office is located at 151 Potrero Avenue, SF, CA 94103. Office hours are Mon., Tues., Thurs. and Fri. 1 p.m. - 4 p.m. and Wed. 9 a.m. - Noon. Program Directories, containing descriptions of the available masters, are available for $6.00. For information, call 863-8661.

Sportin' Life

Clubs

Sporting Clubs, Sites & Arcades

Swimming Pools of SF

Hey Sports! This is a new ALMANAC feature. If you would like your organization listed, please send a letter, membership package or postcard to tell us about your group, club or site to: THE SAN FRANCISCO ALMANAC, *Sportin' Life*, 1657 Waller Street #A, SF, CA 94117-2811, or call us at 1-800-352-5268. We'd be pleased to include you in the next edition. Thanks!

See *BINGO!; Groups & Associations; Books, Paper & Ink* and *Magazine Racks of SF* for more...

Clubs

Alpineer Club
Family & Single Skiing
450 Hearst Ave., SF 94112
334-3732

American Youth Hostels
Golden Gate Council
425 Divisadero Suite 307, SF 94117
863-1444

Associated Sportsmen of CA
281 Sweeney Street, SF 94134
586-2234

The Backgammon Network
(415) 593-9433

Bay Area Triathlon Club
(415) 282-4491

SF Bowling Association
1485 Bayshore, SF 94128
467-8937

Bridge Club of San Francisco
777 Jones Street, SF 94109
776-6949

California Alpine Club
PO Box 42100, SF 94142
334-4619

Cavendish Bridge Club
100 Gough Street, SF 94109
776-6949

Chess Club
57 Post Street, SF 94104
421-2258

Chess Friends of Northern CA
2460 21st Avenue, SF 94116
731-6851

Chinese Sportsman Club
773 Sacramento St., SF 94108
362-9786

Concordia Sport Club
2355 Ocean Avenue, SF 94132
239-9602

Corinthia Yacht Club
PO Box 857, Tiburon 94920
435-4771

Diving Clubs, Central Council
PO Box 779, Daly City 94107
583-8492

California Golf Club
844 W. Orange Ave., SSF 94080
761-0210

San Francisco Golf Club
Junipero Serra Blvd., SF 94132
469-4100

Gymnastic Association
1306 Elmer Street, Belmont 94002
591-8734

Sea Trek (Kayaking)
85 Liberty Ship Way
Sausalito 94965
332-4457

Lake Merced Sailing Club
Boathouse, Skyline & Harding Rd.,
SF 94132
753-1101

San Francisco Model Yacht Club
36 Kennedy Dr., Golden Gate Park,
SF 94118
386-9762

**Outdoors
Unlimited**
UCSF Campus
476-2078

Pacific Rod & Gun Club
520 John Muir Dr., SF 94132
239-9750

Pamakid Runners
1233 Taraval Street, SF 94116
681-2323

St. Francis Yacht Club
The Marina, SF 94123
563-6363

San Francisco Athletic Club
1630 Stockton Street, SF 94133
781-0166

San Francisco Marathon
1233 Taraval Street, SF 94116
681-2324

Scuba, Bamboo Reef Enterprise
584 Fourth Street, SF 94107
362-6694

Sierra Club
730 Polk Street, SF 94109
776-2211

California Soccer Association
1348 Silver Avenue, SF 94134
467-1881

South End Rowing Club
500 Jefferson Street, SF 94109
441-9523 or 885-9564

Special Olympics
741 30th Avenue, SF 94121
221-6575

Sports (Partners) Match
2966 Diamond Street #103, SF 94131
467-9955

SF Tennis Club
645 5th Street, SF 94107
777-9000

Windsurf Berkeley
1827 C 5th Street, Berkeley 94710
(510) 841-9463

Yacht Racing Association
Fort Mason, SF 94123
771-9500

Toastmasters Membership Hotline
(408) 559-3818

Boy Scouts of America
124 Beale Street Ste. 402, SF 94105
543-8780

Society for Barbershop Quartet Singing, PO Box 913, Daly City
826-1717

Sports Car Club of America
1610 Pacific Avenue, SF 94109
775-1010

Dashiell Hammett Society
John's Grill, 63 Ellis Street, SF 94102
986-0069

Gem and Mineral Society
4134 Judah Street, SF 94122
564-4230

Golden Gate Model Railroaders
Randall Museum, Museum Way, SF 94114
863-1399

Philatelic Society of San Francisco
986 Guerrero St., SF 94110
647-7637

African Violet Society
SF County Fair Bldg., GG Park 94122
558-3622

American Fuchsia Society
SF County Fair Bldg., GG Park 94122
558-3623

Cactus & Succulent Society
2659 Post Street, SF 94115
346-8552

Ikebana Society
Hall of Flowers, GG Park, SF 94122
566-2976

San Francisco Garden Club
640 Sutter Street, SF 94102
771-0282

Strybing Arboretum Society
9th Avenue & Lincoln Way
GG Park, SF 94122
661-1316

Sports Clubs & Sites

Center Shot Archery Shop
Sales, Rentals, Lessons
728 La Playa Street (47th & Fulton)
Mondays 1 p.m. - 6 p.m.
Tues.-Sat. 10 a.m. - 6 p.m.
751-2776
(Near GG Park Archery Range)

Musee Mechanique
1090 Point Lobos Avenue (Cliff House)
Vintage Nickelodeons and Automatons

Park Bowl
1855 Haight Street
752-2366
Lanes open daily

SF Batter's Box
(Batting Cage)
Wolf Sporting Goods
4434 Mission Street
585-2000

Belmont Iceland
(Skating Rink)
815 Old County Road, Belmont
592-0532

Berkeley Iceland
(Skating Rink)
2727 Milvia (near Ashby BART)
(510) 843-8800

Rolladium Roller Rink
363 N. Amphlett Blvd.
San Mateo
342-2711

ABC Billiard
233 Turk Street
922-4699

Family Billiards
2807 Geary Blvd.
Daily 11:30 a.m. - 2 a.m.
387-3830

South Beach Billiards
270 Brannan
495-5939

Billiard Palacade
(Billiards & Arcade)
5179 Mission (by Geneva)
585-2331

Great Entertainer
(Billiards & Arcade)
975 Bryant
861-8833

Gamescape
(Darts)
333 Divisadero
621-4263

Ginsberg's Pub
(Darts)
400 Bay
771-3760

Renaissance Ballroom
(Ballroom Dances & Classes)
285 Ellis (across from SF Hilton)
474-0920

Metronome Ballroom
(Dances & Classes)
1830 17th Street
252-9000

Card Rooms

Artichoke Joe's
(Open 24 Hours)
659 Huntington Avenue
San Bruno
589-3145

Oaks Club Room
(Open 24 Hours)
4097 San Pablo Avenue
Emeryville
(510) 653-4456

Cameo Club Card Room
4120 El Camino Rialto
San Bruno
493-5056

Swimming Pools of San Francisco

The SF Recreation and Parks Department operates nine public pools, of which all but one are indoor. (Mission Pool, outdoors, is open summer only.) Each pool has its own schedule of activities and is free. Pick up the *Aquatics Program Guide* at McLaren Lodge (Stanyan and Fell) for ten pages of details. Come in, the water's fine!

North Beach Pool, Lombard & Mason
274-0200

Hamilton Pool, Geary & Steiner
292-2001

Rossi Pool, Arguello & Anza
666-7014

Mission Pool, 19th by Valencia
695-5002

Garfield Pool, 26th & Harrison
695-5001

Sava Pool, 19th & Wawona
753-7000

Balboa Pool, San Jose Ave. & Havelock
337-4701

King Pool, 3rd St. & Carroll Ave.
822-5707

Coffman Pool, Visitacion Ave. & Hahn
337-4702

These pools are available through a membership or fee:

The Sheehan Hotel
620 Sutter (at Mason)
Open to public Mon.-Fri. 7:30 a.m.-7:30 p.m., weekends 10 a.m. - 5 p.m. Fee for use of fully-equipped workout room, locker room and pool is $4.00; discount passes available. Charming heated pool!

Jewish Community Center
3200 California (at Presidio)
Membership required, call 346-6040

Koret Health Center and Pool
University of San Francisco
Parker at Turk
666-6820
Now open to the public weekdays 6 a.m. - 2 p.m., Saturdays 8 a.m. - 2 p.m. and Sundays 10 a.m. - 2 p.m. Cost per use is $6.00, with discount passes available for frequent users. This is a beautiful world-class Olympic-sized pool.

San Francisco Bay Club
One Lombard
Membership required, call 433-2550.

SF Boys & Girls Club
Membership required, call 221-0790.

YMCA
220 Golden Gate Avenue
Membership required, call 885-0460

B-I-N-G-O!

35 Bingo Games in SF

How do you spell good clean fun, a charitable effort and a chance to "hit it big?" **B-I-N-G-O!** Here's a pretty good list of games in San Francisco. The games vary in size and ambiance. A visit or a phone call will tell you if a particular game suits your spirit. Hours given are game-start time. Many halls open the doors for socializers and "early-bird" games prior to these times. By the way, if we've missed your favorite game, or if you'd like us to include more details, as many have this year, please call or write and we'll include it in next year's ALMANAC. Good luck to all of the players!

Filipino-American Council of SF
3416 19th Street
626-0773
Tuesdays, Thursdays 9 p.m.

Filipino Senior Citiz[...]
83 6th Street
495-9423
Thursdays at [...]

Bayview Hunters Point Senior Ctr.
1706 Yosemite Avenue
822-1444
Thursdays at 1 p.m.

Brotherhood Way Jewish Community Center
Admission Fee
All Games Pay Out $250
Sundays at 7 p.m.

Brotherhood Way Armenian Cultural Foundation
825 Brotherhood Way
Admission Buy-In
All Games Pay Out $250
Fridays at 7:15 p.m.

[...] Taraval Street (at 46th Ave.)
664-7375
100–200 Players, Pay Out $250
Thursdays at 7 p.m.

Christian Church of Samoa
260 Sagamore Street
239-9658
Tuesdays at 7 p.m.

Doegler Senior Center (Daly City)
101 Lake Merced
991-8012
Tuesdays at 1:30 p.m.

El Bethel Arms
1234 McAllister Street
921-7614
Wednesdays at 1 p.m.

Eureka Valley Recreation Center
100 Collingwood Street
554-9528
Wednesdays 11 a.m. - 3 p.m.

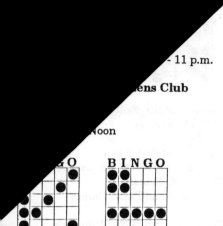

Most Holy Redeemer Support Group
100 Diamond Street
863-6259
More than 20 Games, Admission Fee
Games Pay Out $200
150–350 Players
Sundays at 1 p.m.

Potrero Hill House Seniors
953 DeHaro Street
826-8080
Mon.,Wed., Fri. 12:30 p.m. - 3:30 p.m.

**Recreation Center for the Handi-
capped Parents' Auxiliary Bingo**
207 Skyline Blvd.
(across from Lake)
665-4100
20 Games, 150–300 Players
Games Pay Out $250
Fridays 7 p.m.

Richmond District YMCA Seniors
360 18th Avenue
668-2060
Thursdays and Saturdays at 1 p.m.

Sons of Italy
5051 Mission Street (by Italy Avenue)
586-1316
18 Games Pay Out $250
Admission Buy-In
Sundays at 1 p.m.

St. Anne's Church Bingo
850 Judah Street
759-1506
25 Games, 350–400 Players!
Admission Fee, ½-Off Last Tuesday
Tuesdays at 7 p.m.

- 11 p.m.

ens Club

Noon

Lowell Axe Club
1101 Eucalyptus Drive
566-7900
Big Game
Second Saturday Every Month

Mercy High School Bingo
3250 19th Avenue
334-0525
30 Games, Pay Out $250
150–300 Players
Admission Fee
Third Saturday of Every Month at Noon

Mission Senior Citizens
362 Capp Street
826-0440
Mondays at 1 p.m.

Mission YMCA Senior Center
4080 Mission Street
586-6900
Wednesdays, Fridays at 1 p.m.

St. Anthony's Church
3215 Army Street
647-2704
Tuesdays at 7:30 p.m.

St. Elizabeth's Church
449 Holyoke Street
468-0820
Tuesdays at 7:30 p.m.

St. Ignatius College Preparatory School
2001 37th Avenue
731-7500 (School Only)
Hard and Paper games, Admission Fee
More Than 20 Games, Pay Out $250
200–300 Players
Mondays at 7 p.m.

St. John Armenian Apostolic Church
275 Olympia Way
753-9547
25 Games, Pay Out $250
150–300 Players
Mondays at 7 p.m.

St. Kevin's Parish Church
704 Cortland Avenue
648-5751
Wednesdays at 7:30 p.m.

St. Michael's Catholic Church & School
55 Farallones Street
333-6424
Sundays at 1 p.m.

St. Monica's Church
470 24th Avenue (Hall @ 23rd & Geary)
751-5275
All Games Pay Out $250
100–250 Players
Admission Buy-In
All Paper Games
Fridays at 7 p.m.

St. Patrick's Church
756 Mission Street
421-0547
Sundays at 1:30 p.m.

St. Paul's Church Bingo
221 Valley Street (29th & Church)
648-7538
15 Games Pay Out $230–$250
Admission Fee
Fridays at 7:30 p.m.

St. Paul's Intermediate School
1660 Church
648-2055
Fridays at 7 p.m.

St. Phillip's Church
725 Diamond Street
282-0141
Big Game
Tues. at 7:30 p.m., Sat. at 12:30 p.m.

St. Stephen's Catholic Church
473 Eucalyptus Drive (at 21st Ave.)
681-2444
30 Games Pay Out $250
Admission Buy-In
More Than 250 Players
Fridays at 7 p.m.,
Every First Saturday at Noon

Stonestown YMCA Seniors
333 Eucalyptus Drive
759-9622
Fridays at 1 p.m.

United Irish Societies of SF
2700 45th Avenue
661-2700
150—400 Players
Games Pay Out $250
Wednesdays at 7 p.m.

Bingo Bible

Read *Gambling Times'* **Guide to Bingo,** written by Roger Snowden, franchiser of *Bingo Bugle* newspapers all across America. This book explains arcane bingo lingo, discusses strategies for winning and tells you where to find high-stakes bingo games operated on California Indian reservations. It's available at many local bookstores and at the Main Library.

History of Bingo

Edwin Lowe, a New York toy salesman, dropped into a Jacksonville, Florida carnival in December 1929, possibly to revive his spirits after having chosen The Great Depression to go into business for himself. He witnessed a popular carny game, BEANO, which kept the carnival workers gambling until the wee hours. One carny, a tongue-tied woman, cried out "BINGO" (instead of BEANO) upon filling her card.

This bit of serendipity led Lowe to invent and market the two-dollar Bingo game to great success, eventually developing a mammoth 6,000-card version. The game swept to popularity as a church and club fundraiser during otherwise difficult days. Bill Harrah, who would later build one of the most powerful casino operations in Reno, Lake Tahoe and Las Vegas, began his climb to power with a Venice Beach bingo parlor!

Fun
Day
Trips

China Camp

China Camp State Park is one of most pristine natural watershed regions on The Bay. It is located on the Point San Pedro Peninsula in Marin County, only four miles from San Rafael and Highway 101. Recreational activities abound, including day hikes, picnics and beaches for swimming, boat launching and camping.

The park rests on the site of a turn-of-the-century Chinese shrimping and fishing village that once had a population of 10,000. A small museum pays tribute to the Bay's colorful past.

Shrimping still goes on in this old fishing village. You'll see the old wooden shacks that housed the fishermen and their families, the original fishing pier, the surviving fish preparation areas and more.

A little cafe offers drinks and sandwiches (open weekends only). Campers will find primitive campsites with tables, food-lockers and fire rings. Wood gathering is illegal; bring your own or buy it at the entrance-kiosk if you plan on building a campfire. The campground also offers water and pit toilets; camping requires reservations. Dogs are not allowed on some trails.

For more information about this local oasis, call MISTIX at 1-800-446-7275.

Chinatown Culinary Tours

Shirley Fong-Torres, who comes from a Chinatown restaurant family, has put together the "Wok Wiz" tours of Chinatown. These tours give those interested in Chinese customs and culture a chance to begin exploring this fascinating SF neighborhood.

Shirley and her guides will take you on the "Cooks' tour" of Chinatown that is popular with natives and visitors alike. Prices vary, depending on which tour you choose. You will even visit one of Chinatown's oldest fortune cookie factories! Call 355-9657 for details.

City Guides

City Guides is one of SF's premier walking tour series, led by volunteer guides well-versed in local history and lore. From Art Deco in the Marina to Victorian San Francisco (Lafayette Square), City Guides has a rich variety of outings. A few favorites include the Fire Department Museum, Nob Hill, The Presidio and the Gold Rush City. A popular new tour explores the historic Palace Hotel, under restoration.

Friends of the San Francisco Public Library sponsors this year-long series of tours. Tours are free, but a donation may be given to your guide. Send a self-addressed legal size 29¢-stamped envelope to City Guides, Civic Center, The Main Library, SF, CA, 94102 for a descriptive schedule of tours.

Call City Guides at 557-4266 for more information about walking tours.

Strybing Arboretum

Tired? Frazzled? The Strybing Arboretum, located in Golden Gate Park by Lincoln Way and 9th Avenue, is heartily recommended as a little oasis of peace and quiet in this fast-paced City.

If you want to know more about the plants you're looking at, short tours of this garden of gardens leave weekdays at 1:30 p.m., with weekend tours beginning at 10:30 a.m. and 1:30 p.m. Tours are free.

These tours emphasize seasonal features of the gardens. The Arboretum greenery is looking good after a wet Spring this past year. The Arboretum Bookstore is a treat, too.

Golden Gate Park Tours

Friends of Recreation and Parks' walking tours are held May through October. Tours are at 11 a.m. Saturdays and 11 a.m. and 2 p.m. Sundays. Tours are held rain or shine.

Saturday's Strawberry Hill tour meets at the park map by the Japanese Tea Garden and includes the Music Concourse area, Stow Lake and Strawberry Hill, among other park sites. A tour of the east end of the Park is held on Sundays at 11 a.m. The tour includes some little-known areas of the Park, including the De Laveaga Dell, the horseshoe courts and the Fuchsia Garden. This tour highlights the Children's Playground and the Music Concourse, too.

A tour of the west end of the Park is held on the first Sunday of the month at 2 p.m. Meet at the Park map at Spreckels Lake (36th Avenue); the tour includes the stables, the windmills and the buffalo paddocks. Other tours include the Japanese Tea Garden and a neat once-a-month tour of Lloyd Lake. Call 221-1311 for information.

A tour of Stern Grove is held on the second Saturday of the month. Meet at the entrance to Stern Grove at 19th Avenue and Sloat to learn more about this beautiful forest park, including the SF Trocadero Roadhouse.

Friends of the Urban Forest Walking Tours

Join FUF for their fantastic guided tours of City neighborhoods. Tree tours offer a varied palate of urban sights and sensations to capture the interest of the gardener, the nature lover, the sightseer and the SF history buff. Call FUF for details at 543-5000. Recommended (see also *ALMANAC Green*).

Here's the 1992 FUF schedule:

Bernal Heights
w/ Cheri Kollin
Saturday April 25, 10 a.m. - Noon
Meet in Triangle Park
at Coleridge and Coso

Golden Gate Park
w/ Linda Liebelt
Saturday May 9, 10 a.m. - Noon
Meet at Strybing Arboretum entrance

Embarcadero
w/ Bill Carney
Wednesday June 24, Noon - 1 p.m.
Meet at Vaillancourt Fountain, Justin Herman Plaza, at the foot of Market St.

Parnassus Heights
w/ Linda Liebelt
Saturday June 13, 10 a.m. - Noon
Meet at UC Medical Center, Milberry Union, 500 Parnassus

Russian Hill
w/ Lin Galea
Saturday August 22, 10 a.m. - Noon
Meet at corner of Francisco & Polk

Dolores Park
w/ Lin Galea
Saturday September 19, 10 a.m. - Noon
Meet at 19th Street & Sanchez

Filbert Street Steps
w/ Cheryl Kollin
Saturday October 3, 10 a.m. - Noon
Meet at the entrance to Coit Tower

Lyon Street Steps
w/ Lin Galea
Saturday October 24, 10 a.m. - Noon
Meet at Broadway & Divisadero

Deco Visions in The City

The Art Deco Society of California gives walking tours highlighting the best examples in Deco architecture and design, history and preservation efforts. The Society has a two-pronged goal; to educate about Deco and to preserve it. Society memberships are encouraged and bring you *The Sophisticate*, the group's stylish bi-annual magazine. Each June the Society sponsors Art Deco Weekend-by-the-Bay, a mixed bag of jazzy events throughout The City. For walking tour info, memberships or the Spring event, call 982-DECO.

Victorian Trails

The Foundation for San Francisco's Architectural Heritage, a local group dedicated to the preservation and re-use of architecturally and historically significant buildings, offers an ongoing Pacific Heights walking tour series, Sundays at 12:30 p.m.

The tour concentrates on area Victorians and costs just $3.00. Membership in SF Heritage brings their entertaining and informative newsletter. Call 441-3004 for information.

Open Studios
Fall Art Harvest

Here's a fun way to spend a pleasant Fall day. During three weekends each Autumn, the public is invited into the studios of more than 500 local artists.

Unlike the commercial setting of a gallery or the formal setting of a museum, the Open Studios weekends provide a fun, behind-the-scenes look at San Francisco's energetic arts community. Last year more than 20,000 people participated in this free annual Bay Area tradition.

In 1992 the Open Studios program will take place on three consecutive weekends: October 31–November 1, November 7–8 and November 14–15. The event is organized with a directory and map to make visiting studios of your choice easy. A more exact photo/review directory of each artist and their work is available. An exhibition and a juried competition are also held in conjunction with this event.

This is a relaxed, enriching opportunity for artists and art lovers to meet, chat and enjoy themselves.

Call Artspan at 861-9838 to receive the directory for SF and the Bay Area. Artspan is a project sponsored by California Lawyers for the Arts and corporate and private supporters of the arts.

Farallon Islands Voyage

The Farallon Islands excursions from June through November allow for a rare opportunity to see these isolated Pacific islands that lie just a stone's throw off our coast. The islands and the ocean around them are a welcome sanctuary for whales, dolphins and a variety of sea birds. You'll board an 85-foot vessel at San Francisco Yacht Harbor and be in the charge of highly-skilled naturalists.

The trip takes you sailing under the Golden Gate Bridge and north up the coast. Call well ahead for weekend reservation schedule. Dress warmer 'n ever for this one and bring binoculars. Reservation brings a complete information packet. These full-day trips are held on weekends and select Fridays.

Call Oceanic Society Expeditions for details at 474-3385. Tours about $55. Great way to spend a special day!

The *Original* San Francisco Roommate Referral™ Service

*Serving All of San Francisco
Since 1975*

**$23 Fee
List Your Vacancy Free**

*Always Over 300 Current
Shared Rentals Available!*

**Call 626-0606
Open 7 Days a Week**

**610A Cole Street (near Haight)
San Francisco, CA 94117**

Ask Your Friends About Us!™

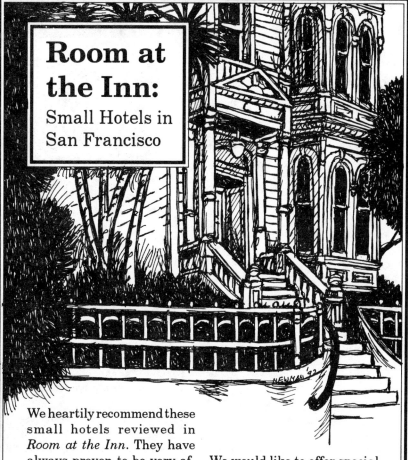

Room at the Inn:
Small Hotels in San Francisco

We heartily recommend these small hotels reviewed in *Room at the Inn*. They have always proven to be very affordable and our family and friends have found them truly enjoyable. They also like THE ALMANAC, and have shown their support in many ways. We encourage you to stay at one of these hotels the next time you come to The City.

We would like to offer special thanks to Ingrid Summerfield at the Sheehan Hotel; Tom & Robert Field and Bonnie Lee Berg at The San Remo Hotel and Deborah Brady at Brady Acres for their support of our growing local publication.

Brady Acres

Brady Acres is a small, intimate hotel just three blocks northwest of Union Square, between Post and Geary, on Jones. Guests prefer staying at Brady Acres because of the competitive prices and the emphasis on personal service. The hotel was recently remodeled, each room being appointed in its own distinctive style. It is located in a very central neighborhood, convenient to many of The City's downtown activities.

Brady Acres offers amenities such as free local telephone service, a personal answering machine, fully equipped wet bars, coffee maker, refrigerator, toaster, television and even cassette stereo. Brady Acres has on-site laundry facilities, FAX and copy machine ready for guests. Parking is available at a nearby garage at preferred rates. The friendly management is available to help you arrange any special services you may require during your stay.

Single rooms run $50–$55 a night, with double rooms $60–$65. Inquire about special weekly rates available year-round.

Sheehan Hotel

The Sheehan Hotel offers affordable comfort in the tradition of fine small European hotels. The Sheehan's historic facade imparts The City's rich architectural heritage. The hotel's location, two blocks from Union Square and just below Nob Hill, is ideal for business or pleasure in The City, in a neighborhood rich with cafes, bookstores, galleries and theatres.

The classic swimming pool (the largest heated indoor hotel pool in The City) is a real delight, popular with City residents. The adjoining fitness room is well equipped for a workout. The Sheehan's lobby Tea Room offers great coffee, tea, home-baked scones and light fare. Each room is equipped with cable TV and private phones. Cars can be parked at reduced rates at the garage across the street.

The fine Sheehan Hotel is an ideal home base for touring San Francisco. With the cable cars, Union Square, Chinatown, Nob Hill and more nearby, you will spend your special time in a neighborhood many San Franciscans would love to call home!

Room rates range from $40–$95, depending on type. Included is a continental breakfast buffet, featuring home-baked goods.

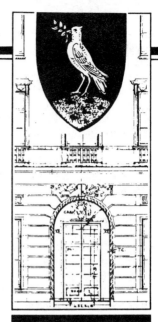

SHEEHAN

Affordable Comfort in the Heart of San Francisco

■ ■

620 Sutter St.
San Francisco, CA
415/775-6500

1-800-848-1529

The San Remo Hotel

The San Remo Hotel is a family owned and operated Italianate Victorian Hotel located in the Fisherman's Wharf/North Beach area. The hotel, constructed in 1906, was recently restored to its original period charm. Antique beds, claw-foot tubs, lace curtains, polished floors and redwood wainscotting speak to her elegant and historic past. At one time her north wall faced Water Street, the original bayfront, before the waterline moved far to the north.

Many of the guest rooms offer views of The City's world famous landmarks, including Coit Tower, Nob Hill, Russian Hill and a modern trademark, the Transamerica Pyramid. The cable cars, just a stone's throw away, can whisk you in true San Francisco style to many of The City's nearby sights.

After a day of fun or business, return to The San Remo's restored restaurant, featuring family-style continental fare and a bar shipped around Cape Horn over a century ago. The piano bar and cocktail lounge are local favorites.

Rates are $35–$85 per night; weekly rates are available. One of SF's most affordable and rustic/elegant historic hotels, close to the sights of The City.

Look for the 1941 "Woody" station wagon parked faithfully out front!

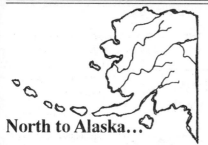

North to Alaska...

The 6th edition of the *Bed and Breakfast Homes Directory* by Diane Knight is $10.95 from Windham Bay Press at Box 1198, Occidental, CA 95465. Order it from Windham Bay by phone at (707) 823-7150. The book includes many favored B&B's in the $45–$65 range. It features cozy stops in California, Oregon, Washington and even British Columbia. Descriptions and photos of each stay are included.

Windham Bay also offers Alaska's *Inside Passage Traveler*, which will guide you through the inland waterway's extensive ferry system. The author, Ellen Searby, worked for the ferries for fifteen years and promises time-tested inside advice on this most affordable way to see Alaska.

The Californias Bed & Breakfast Directory is a free booklet that features short reviews of hundreds of California B&B's. It is published by Yellow Brick Road for the California Department of Tourism. Call (916) 327-3391 to receive a copy. A rich resource for all California travelers and residents!

Bed & Breakfast/ Small Hotel Reservation Services

Here are reservation services to help you find a good small hotel or B&B in California.

Bed & Breakfast International
PO Box 282910
San Francisco, CA 94128-2910
1-800-872-4500
B&B's in Northern California

Golden Gate Reservations
(415) 771-6915
Better small hotels in SF

Country Inns/Russian River
PO Box 2416
Guerneville, CA 95446
1-800-927-4667
B&B's in the Russian River region

B&B San Francisco
PO Box 420009
San Francisco, CA 94142
1-800-452-8249
B&B's in the SF, Carmel, Monterey areas

Bed & Breakfast Exchange
1458 Lincoln Avenue
Calistoga, CA 94515
1-800-942-2924
B&B's in Napa, Sonoma, Mendocino

Cohost America's B&B
PO Box 9302
Whittier, CA 90608
(213) 699-8427
California home stays

"Napa" means plenty in the local Indian dialect. The Napa Valley growing region is 30-miles-long and stretches from the Mayacamas range on the West to the shores of Lake Berryessa to the East. The 30,000 low-yielding grape vineyard acres of the valley yield only about four percent of the State's wine. Quality, not quantity, is generally the focus of the Napa Valley growers. The vintages from this beautiful coastal valley are known the world over.

Highway 29 is the main artery through Napa. It is reached via Highway 101 over the Golden Gate Bridge. It will take you about an hour to get up to the Valley, where some 75 wineries will be open for visits. Lunch, wine-tasting and other diversions await you. There is so much to see, and so much wine to drink, that many choose to make a weekend of it, staying in one of the many bed & breakfasts that dot the rich grower's region.

Plan Your Wine Tour

To have the richest visit possible, do a little reading first. Call The Wine Institute (the growers' association) at (415) 512-0151 to order their free map, *Wineries of the Napa Valley*. This beautiful full-size color winery roadmap features more than seventy growers and relates the history and an overview of the Valley. The next thing you'll need is a guidebook...

The below Napa Valley Wine Guide was found at The Booksmith in The Haight, and is available at Brentano's, Waldenbooks, Green Apple Books and others. (See *Magazine & Booksellers of SF* for telephone numbers of these bookstores in The City to call and check stock).

Cole's Insider Guide to Wines and Vines of Napa County, written by Austin Moss and published by Brete Harrison, both native Napa Valley area residents, offers short reviews of most of the wineries and their wines. Although the reviews are bare-bones, primarily focusing on the wines and winemakers, the $11.95 book offers an excellent guide to the Napa Valley wineries open to the general public. A back-page foldout map highlights each location. There is a winery appendix, too, explaining the trade vernacular you will hear from friendly workers at each location and defining the varieties of Napa Valley wines.

Bay Area Graphics & Printing Co.

Friendly Peter Chong, owner of Bay Area Graphics and Printing Co., offers a
neighborhood printing service that aims to please. Peter offers quality design
and printing for the full spectrum of business needs, including letterhead and
logos, business cards, envelopes and labels. His business is built upon satisfied
customers. He has a talent for helping his customers solve printing problems
with affordable, creative and quality approaches to their printing needs.

Heavenly Maids!

If you're moving in or out of an apartment, home or business, organizing a party or dinner or leaving town for business or a vacation, you've got enough to do. For party clean-up, carpet cleaning, ironing, stove and refrigerator maintenance, mini-blind and wall washing and other domestic chores, call the Heavenly Maids. Sit back and enjoy a little bit of heaven right here on earth. You've certainly earned it!

BUILDING A BUSINESS?

Call Business Exchange International of San Francisco (BXI)!

Barter your skills & products in exchange for the skills of others! Build up "trade dollars" that can be exchanged later for services.

Virtually anything can be bartered or bartered for, including:

- Accounting
- Computers
- FAXes
- Contracting
- Much More . . .

BXI is the world's oldest and largest trade club for business owners and professionals.

Call (415) 227-0480 for a free start-up package, today!

Art Bonner's Art-Tistic Interiors

Art-Tistic Interiors is Art Bonner's full-service upholstery, drapery and fabrics service in The Richmond (just blocks from the ocean). Art set out in 1962 to supply affordable slip-covers to a growing community of home furniture restorers. Over the past thirty years, he has become accomplished in every facet of this skillful business. Whether you're re-upholstering a fun thrift-shop chair or sofa or you're a designer handling an entire home, Art offers the entire range of upholstery, bed coverings, drape and curtain services. He has contributed his considerable experience and friendly skills to restaurants, fine homes and hotels, home shows and more. No job is too big or too small for Art Bonner's Art-Tistic Interiors. Give Art a call for your next upholstery task.

Next time you're at the bookstore, check for Sunset Books' titles Slipcovers and Bedspreads *and* Furniture Upholstery. *Art Bonner designed and crafted the hundreds of examples included in these national do-it-yourself best-sellers. Art has done yacht interiors, too, and once even designed a custom slip-cover for a 1956 T-Bird convertible! Free estimates offered at his place or yours. Call 386-8511.*

Omega Television

Those of us who saw the recent *20/20* exposé on repair services will be pleased to know about Omega Television, Dan Bennett and Don Adams' highly trusted repair service. Omega Television has been in business for 17 years. When your television, VCR or stereo receiver breaks down, you'll receive reliable repair service at a reasonable price.

Omega TV's repeat customers will testify to the quality and honesty of their service, the fast turn-around time and the accuracy of their estimates. A typical repair takes 1–3 days. Bring in your TV or VCR for a free estimate and you'll receive low-key, no-pressure diagnostics and advice.

One long-time customer says, "I like them and I've used them for years. They get right to it. If they can't fix it, they don't charge you a penny." Another adds, "They fix things fast, and you don't have to go back. We've bought several TV's and VCR's from Omega. Their prices are competitive and you get terrific service, as well. They have earned, and maintained, our trust."

VCR tune-ups are a specialty. Omega TV offers VCR cleanings and adjustments at very reasonable prices. Omega is open Mon.-Sat. 10 a.m. - 6 p.m. Call 826-0732 for friendly service.

Chiropractic

By Dr. R. Arles Tooker, D.C.

Chiropractic principles are not new by any means. This science of treating the human condition (G. *cheir*, hand and *prakticos*, practitioner) was practiced by the Egyptians, the Greeks and the American Indians, as well as others, well before the birth of Christ. As a Western science, it was founded by D.D. Palmer in 1895. Palmer created a methodology for adjustment of the vertebrae; that method is called *chiropractic*.

Today the practice of chiropractic is well established as a valid method of health care. Chiropractic does not deal with the effects of a disease and it does not guess, surmise or theorize as to treatment. It recognizes the premise that normal health is possible only when the central nervous system is working properly and the spine is well adjusted.

The central nervous system directs all of the systems of the body. This all-important network passes impulses through the spinal cord to every organ, tissue and cell. These nerves branch off and leave the spinal cord through openings between movable bones of the spine, known as vertebrae. When the nerves are "pinched," impulses are restricted from their specific tasks. These *subluxations* cause ill health.

The chiropractor locates the impinged nerves and then gently adjusts the misaligned vertebrae into place. When these vertebrae are again properly aligned, full health and comfort can follow. Today, at least six years of highly-specialized training is required to graduate and earn licensure (D.C.) Hundreds of hours of training in basic sciences such as anatomy, physiology, pathology and diagnosis are included in the D.C.'s extensive formal education and training.

Experience has shown that acute and chronic back and neck pain, painful joints and recurring headaches, among other painful ailments, respond well to the specialized care offered by the modern-day chiropractic professional.

———————— ————————

Dr. Arles Tooker (pronounced just like Charles without the "ch") and Dr. Eric Frankel share a partnership at 2369 Ocean Avenue. Dr. Tooker uses the technique of C.S. Gonstead, an internationally-known pioneer in the field. He graduated Cum Laude from Palmer Chiropractic College West after spending his earliest years instructing in Bay Area schools. He is very comfortable working with young people, as well as adults. For appointments call 587-7000. First-time courtesy examinations are available.

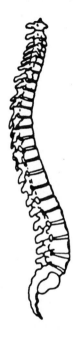

TRUE BLUE CAFE

Salvatore Bovoso
Stefen Reilly

8 am - 1:45 pm
Daily
Closed Wednesday

And Smile, Darn 'Ya, Smile!

 522 JONES PRINTED USA **SF CA 94102** ☎ **415 885.2767**

Dottie's True Blue Cafe

Dottie's True Blue Cafe is a San Francisco breakfast dream—perfect prices, a colorful mixed clientele and truly delicious all-day breakfasts. This Mom-and-Pop City diner was created by Salvatore Bovoso and Stefen Reilly. Sal and Stefen (the executive chef at Asta) offer hungry customers personalized service with a big morning smile. "I know how 30 different customers like their eggs cooked," brags Sal. A true-blue tribute to Stefen's first boss Dottie Denmark, who gave the twelve-year-old Reilly his first job at her luncheonette in Queens, Dottie's offers the best pancakes and eggs in town. The restaurant is located in an upbeat Tenderloin neighborhood rich with small hotels, magazine stands and other after-breakfast adventures. (Can be quite busy Sundays early.)

Breakfast is served from 8 a.m. until 1:45 p.m. (closed Wednesdays) with lunch fare from 11:30 a.m. on. *"Food, Three Stars..."*

—*Patricia Unterman, SF Chronicle.*

Tandoori Cookery

A *tandoor* is shaped much like the huge jar in which Ali Baba hid from the Forty Thieves. The tandoor pot is usually sunk neck-deep in the ground, or, if built above the ground, is heavily insulated with thick plaster. It is then heated with red-hot coals.

The best known of the *tandoori* dishes is a chicken preparation for which broilers are skinned and the meat of the breast and legs carefully cut in slits. The meat is then sprinkled with salt and lime juice and marinated for at least 12 hours. The marinade is a mixture of well-beaten curds and a *masala* of ground ginger, garlic, green and red chiles and sometimes saffron. The chickens are speared on thin iron strips that are placed in the tandoor, which has hot, evenly heated sides.

Tradition holds that a tandoor in regular use improves the flavor of anything cooked in it, for the heated clay releases a mellow fragrance that permeates the food. More flavor is added to the chicken by the smoke that comes from the dripping of the marinade onto the hot coals of the tandoor.

Gaylord Restaurant *at Ghirardelli Square features tandoori dishes, along with vegetarian specialties and delicious curry dishes. Their award-winning food and top service await you...*

180

Pacific Framing Company

Pacific Framing owner Eric Saul comes to the framing trade from a museum background. Eric served as Director of The Presidio Museum, and remains heavily involved with SF's arts and historic preservation community. In the 1980s he led a planning project to help The City begin to establish a municipal history museum. (After exhaustive work in creating a museum working plan, no Chamber of Commerce business was found to contribute a suitable space.)

Look no further than Pacific Framing for top-quality framing and a huge collection of 3,000 frame styles for your treasured paintings, posters and art.

Dr. Clean Means It...

Dr. Clean has been providing cleaning services to residential and commercial customers since February 1988. The good doctor, owner Bill Carlton, offers customized cleaning programs for small businesses, apartment/condominium complexes, tenant vacancies and homes and apartments.

A dozen trained cleaners and a small and highly organized support staff provide reasonably priced and professional service, including all equipment and supplies. "Latch-key" service allows Dr. Clean to operate when no one is home to let the cleaner in. Keys are tightly retained for security. All cleaners are regular Dr. Clean employees, too, protecting customers from liability for worker's comp., tax reporting and insurance, often extra issues with many "independent" contractors.

How clean is it? Dr. Clean means clean, making customer satisfaction and convenience their top priority and working extra hard to keep you pleased. The good doctor is as proud of the work of his roaming staff as you are of your home, shop or business location.

Next time you're looking for a top-notch cleaning service, call Dr. Clean, "your prescription for care-free cleaning." Call 474-3345 for friendly information.

Thanks!

Special thanks to these recommended
businesses that sponsored *Service with a Smile.*

Your considerate patronage of THE SAN FRANCISCO ALMANAC
helps make this publication possible for everyone in the
community...

Editor,
Walter Biller

If you would like your business reviewed for inclusion in next year's issue of THE
SAN FRANCISCO ALMANAC, contact Walter Biller at 1-800-352-5268 or 751-0657 in
The City. Traditionally we publish in July. It is best to call well before March.

24-Hour World

Late-Night Services

Full-Service Post Office
Road #6 SF Airport
I-280 (San Bruno Ave. Exit),
Cross Overpass onto S. Airport Blvd.,
Make Right onto Airport Access Rd.
742-1406 Open 24 hours

Video Rental
Video Cafe/Geary & 21st Ave.
387-3999 Open 24 hours

Computer/Copy Center
Kinko's Copies
Behind Stonestown Mall
566-0572 Open 24 hours

Veterinarian
Pets Unlimited
2343 Fillmore (at Washington)
563-6700 Open 24 hours

Flowers
Pinelli's Flowerland
714 Clement
751-4142 Open until 9 p.m.

Grocery Stores, 24 Hours
Cala Foods
(Several—Consult Telephone Book)

Sundries
Walgreen's/Haight & Fillmore
621-6892 Open until Midnight

Locksmiths
All City Locksmith
445 Natoma
495-7217 Service 24 hours

Fitness Center
24-Hour Nautilus
1335 Sutter
776-2200

Laundromat
Little Hollywood Laundromat
1906 Market/252-9357
Open 7 a.m. - Midnight

Car Wash
Self-Service Car Wash
2895 Geary (at Collins)/824-9500
Bring Quarters or $1 Bills
Office: Mon.-Fri. 8 a.m. - 5 p.m.

GOOD SERVICE GUIDE

A SOURCEBOOK OF RECOMMENDED BUSINESSES

Arbor Vitae

1176 Shafter Avenue
San Francisco
822-5520

Don't take those trees in your garden or along your sidewalk for granted. For many of them, San Francisco is not their usual habitat. Far from home, their roots often buried under cement, city trees need extra loving care.

Arbor Vitae *(Latin, Tree of Life)* is San Francisco's leading tree service. Since 1978, Arbor Vitae has offered expert pruning and removal, as well as pest control for insects. They can help keep your trees in top condition by timely fertilization and preventive maintenance. "A healthy tree provides its own first line of defense," says owner and Certified Arborist Ed Brennan. "With routine check-ups, we can head off most problems before they occur."

Annual or quarterly check-ups include deep-root fertilization, soil aeration and pruning and spraying to eliminate bugs, fungi and mildew. Arbor Vitae specializes in disease diagnosis and treatment. Their crews are prompt, professionally attired and fully-insured. They also pride themselves on their clean-up work; they do not leave a mess behind.

Arbor Vitae protects your trees and preserves your patch of the urban forest.

Chula Productions

2325 Third Street, Ste. 430
San Francisco
621-0166

Does the concept of a kitchen mean more than just cooking to you? Before hiring a contractor or doing it yourself, talk to a specialist in this area of home remodeling. Chula Camp is one of SF's leading kitchen and bath designers. She is very active in the design community, organizing special events and seminars at the Design Centers and lecturing at local colleges. Chula's kitchen and bath projects and articles are regularly found in consumer and trade publications.

"Many people are overwhelmed by the idea of a major remodeling project," says Chula. "They wonder where to begin, what's involved, how to find contractors and what it's going to cost."

"We offer design a la carte. We help juggle aesthetics with your budget. I'm like a coach," says Chula. "I can show you how to put together a winning team, help with design, recommend architects and contractors, minimize construction inconvenience. A kitchen isn't just a kitchen anymore. It's often the heart and soul of the home."

GAUTHIER & HALLETT

341A 27TH AVENUE
SAN FRANCISCO
221-1022

EARTHQUAKE CONSTRUCTION SERVICE

522 63RD STREET
OAKLAND
1-800-369-1212

Before you embark on that large home remodeling project, call on architects Gauthier and Hallett. Most architects prefer to design from the ground up, but Gauthier and Hallett specialize in houses and residential remodeling. "We do residential work because we choose to," says Harvard-trained architect Michael Hallett. "It's much more fulfilling than commercial work."

Michael and his wife and partner, Mary-Lynn Gauthier, have helped many San Francisco homeowners achieve their goals in harmony with neighbors and City planning and codes. They begin with an interview and follow up with a proposed contract.

If you decide to work with them, they take the time to listen to your ideas and goals. They research and explain code restrictions, the practical particulars of your home and the choices you need to make. Then they get to work on solving the problem. "A good residential project usually results from a successful collaboration between owners and designers," says Michael. "We don't force our preferences on the owner. We offer creative solutions."

Are you courting financial ruin? If you haven't had your home throughly reinforced and secured to its foundation, you risk losing your entire home investment in the next big earthquake. For between $1,000–$6,000, Earthquake Construction Service can dramatically improve your home's chances of riding out the next major tremor.

Owner James Gillett has seismically reinforced and retrofitted hundreds of SF homes during the last ten years, probably more than any other contractor. He's not one of those instant experts who appeared after the Loma Prieta earthquake in 1989. "This work is relatively inexpensive," says Jim. "And it has proven to be very effective in reducing catastrophic property loss. But it must be done right."

"The amount of bad retrofit work we see is very frightening to us," says Jim, an enthusiatic geologist. "We are often called in to correct others' errors."

187

PHIL'S ELECTRIC COMPANY

2701 LOMBARD STREET
SAN FRANCISCO
921-3776

SANTANA PLUMBING

1475 DOLORES STREET
SAN FRANCISCO
641-4740

Here's a repair store whose customers can't help but sing its praises. "It sounds corny, but it's true," says Vicki Evans, co-owner of Phil's Electric with her husband Bob. "Not a day goes by that someone doesn't come in and say what a great store we have. It's good to know that people value what we're doing."

Bob and two repair technicians repair old vacuum cleaners, toasters, electric shavers and other appliances. "In an emergency we can sometimes fix a small appliance in one day," says Vicki, "Our usual turnaround is 3–5 days."

If your old toaster has lost its spark and Bob thinks that repairing it would cost more than it's worth, he won't charge you for the time spent diagnosing the problem. If replacement is your only option, Vicki and Bob also sell new appliances. "We only carry products with a proven track record for reliability, which are well warrantied by a reputable company," Vicki says. Bob and Vicki are proud of their citywide reputation for good, honest work.

Grace Santana's professional credo is simple—Plumbing With a Smile. No sour-faced workers who stomp through your home, leaving a mess in their wake. Grace and her employees make it a priority to keep their spirits up, and help keep yours up, too!

"We leave your home the way we found it," says Grace. "We wear clean clothes, we do a thorough job and we don't dirty up the house." She arrives most promptly for appointments and quickly gets back to clients with estimates.

Grace has been a popular residential plumbing contractor for ten years, after spending five years as a pipe-fitter on commercial buildings in the Financial District. She does everything from minor repairs to installing hot water heaters and heating units and doing major remodeling projects. Grace admits she is happiest with full remodeling jobs, but is quick to get out and fix a leaky faucet, too.

"I like the small projects as much as the big ones," she says.

TREE LOVERS FLOORS

664 NATOMA STREET
SAN FRANCISCO
863-6833

THE URBAN FARMER STORE

2833 VICENTE STREET
SAN FRANCISCO
661-2204

Bay Area homeowners are taking a renewed shine to hardwood floors. The natural beauty and resilience of hardwood is starting to outstrip its longtime rival, wall-to-wall carpeting. SF's leading hardwood floor company is Tree Lovers Floors.

Over the past 15 years, Tree Lovers has installed or refinished hardwood floors in some of the Bay Area's finest homes. "Our clients demand the highest quality workmanship," says Christopher Hildreth, general manager of the company. "We aren't the cheapest outfit in town—highly skilled craftsmen never are—but we're known as one of the best. We work to a tight schedule and we stay on the job until it's finished. We don't quit until the customer is 100% satisfied."

On new floors, Tree Lovers carefully distributes the lengths according to color and texture. Choose from open-grain woods including oak, ash, elm or walnut, or close-grained maple, birch, beech or pine. Tree Lovers will then enhance the wood's natural beauty, tone and depth. They also do parquets. Free advice, just call.

Keep your garden green—and save precious water—with an automatic watering system from The Urban Farmer, SF's specialists in landscape watering and lighting systems. Whether you use a conventional sprinkler system or just wave a hose around occasionally, you run the risk of overwatering your plants, or letting them die of thirst. Trees, plants and shrubs have different water needs, therefore the problem of making the most of every drop becomes even more difficult.

A drip irrigation system from The Urban Farmer is an electronically-controlled, customized watering system, which delivers exactly the right amount of water to each plant, shrub or flower bed. Once it's set up, you can forget about it; the system runs by itself.

At The Urban Farmer Store in the Sunset District you can see a wide range of plant supplies and tools, and learn more about drip irrigation and lighting systems for your home.

THE GOOD SERVICE GUIDE

A SMART LOCAL PUBLISHER:
ANDREW BARTHOLOMEW

Publisher Andrew Bartholomew created *The Good Service Guide(s)* in 1986. Since then, he and his associates at Guideline Publications have created a valuable resource that features the top services and referrals for Bay Area homeowners.

After relocating from London in the early 1980s, Bartholomew worked on a number of magazines and newspapers in Portland and SF. "I enjoyed the magazine trade, but wanted to do something more useful—more pragmatic. *The Good Service Guide* has proven so. We receive letters and phone calls all the time, thanking us for our work and asking us to send the latest booklets."

The Good Service Guide is sent to thousands of homeowners in Contra Costa, Oakland/Berkeley and San Francisco each year. Great local resource.

Due to space limits, we were not able to include all the GSG/SF reviews, or the customer comments that accompany each article. Call Guideline Publications at (415) 495-3183 to order your copy of *The Good Service Guide.*

Corner, Market & Castro Streets, 1944

Getting Around Town

CityTravel

NEWMAN '92

BART

(Bay Area Rapid Transit)

This 72-mile system was built in the 1960s to provide commuter transit for an expanding Bay Area. It has proved an invaluable asset, serving as a model for new train systems all over the world.

The system today includes 34 stations in four counties and is expanding. BART crosses the Bay through the BART/Transbay Tunnel, which is built in 57 double-tubular sections, sunk 130 feet below the water's surface. The trains reach an average speed of 80 mph. Each car seats 75 people; over 440 cars make up the fleet. All BART riders will attest to the comfort of the seating, which can provide for quiet reading moments and cat naps!

Operating hours are:
Mon.-Fri. 4 a.m. - Midnight
Sat. 6 a.m. - Midnight
Sun. 8 a.m. - Midnight

Call 788-BART for holiday schedules, special event schedules and connections with other transit systems.

The four BART lines are color-coded. Only two lines operate at night and on Sundays, but all destinations can be reached from any station. Fares range from 80¢ for in-city BART use to a maximum fare of $2.65 for trips to the furthest outlying stations.

To enter the BART system, purchase a farecard from the machines available at all stations. Machines are of two types; one type will not give change back. Farecards "remember" their value and addfare machines are available at all station exits. Do not fold or bend your magnetic farecard or you will render it unusable. BART station agents at exits can assist you with any questions you might have.

BART–Bus Transfer

Fremont / Union City
793-BART
Hayward / San Leandro
783-BART
Livermore / Pleasanton
462-BART
Oakland / Berkeley
465-BART
Richmond / El Cerrito
236-BART
SF / Daly City
788-BART
South SF / San Bruno
873-BART
Walnut Creek / Concord
933-BART
Antioch / Pittsburg
754-BART
TTY Transfer Info
839-2220

Here's more BART information:

BART to Amtrak, transfer at Richmond Station. Call Amtrak at 1-800-872-7245 for information. Amtrak can also be boarded via buses to the Oakland Depot. Buses leave The City from The Transbay Terminal at 1st & Mission Streets. (Amtrak does not enter SF Peninsula.)

BART to Oakland Int'l Airport Shuttle bus departs the Coliseum Station every 10 minutes. Fare $1.00.

Frequency of BART trains:
Monday-Friday 4 a.m. - 5 a.m., trains leave every 30 minutes;
Monday-Friday 5 a.m. - 7 p.m., trains leave every 15 minutes;
Monday-Friday 7 p.m. - Midnight, all-day Saturday and Sunday, trains leave every 20 minutes. Allow for this time.

Bikes on BART: A BART Bike Permit allows you to bring your bike onto the trains during weekday non-commute hours and all-day weekends. Call the BART Bikeline at 467-7127 to order an application. For information on bike peak-hour commuting, see *CALTRANS Bike Shuttle* on Page 199.

Passes: BART offers a wide range of commuter, senior, disabled and youth passes. Call 464-7133 for information.

Buy a **BART/Muni Map**. Best deal in town! Just $1.50 at many locations.

The Muni System

It all began after The Gold Rush, with five privately-owned cable-car lines and a horse-drawn route. Around the turn of the century, there were no less than 12 separately owned-and-operated transit services.

To make a long story short, in 1944 it all became one: Muni. This system carries 250-million riders each year and has a stop located within two blocks of 95% of City residences.

The Clay Street Hill Railroad—1873

Canon Kip door-to-door vans in San Francisco for registered elderly and disabled/wheelchair passengers available 8:30 a.m. - 5 p.m. Weekdays. Pick-up requests can be made three days in advance. Special hours charter services are also available. Call 931-3933 for information and subsidized fares.

Cable Cars

Powell & Hyde Street
Line began in 1873.

San Francisco's cable cars began service in 1873. They were developed by Andrew Halladie, a San Francisco wire manufacturer. At one time, there were many cable car lines in operation. The system proved to be very popular among the "hob-nobs," the early "settlers" of Nob Hill.

After three years of work, the restoration of the three remaining lines was completed in 1984. They remain *the* way to commute for many locals.

The cable cars have a unique and very important set of rules. Only two standees are allowed between the posts on the running boards. Hold on most securely when rounding curves. Do not extend hands, legs or baggage out from car exterior. Wait for cable cars to stop completely before boarding or disembarking. Stay off of the yellow-painted floorspace, as this marks the working area of the crew. Tell the conductor or gripman when you wish to stop; they'll do so at the next opportunity.

If you like downhill rides best, take the Hyde Street car to Fisherman's Wharf. This hill has the steepest grade, 21.3%, although no matter how fast it seems, top speed remains nine miles per hour. Fare is $3.00. It's really fun!

Muni LRV's
(Light Rail Vehicles)

Muni LRV's serve five lines in SF, all of which run along the Market Street subway line and terminate at Embarcadero Station near the Ferry Building. The LRV's are part of the regular Muni system; fares, passes and transfers are the same as those on buses. Thirty-five Breda Costruzionia Ferroviare trains from Pistoia, Italy will arrive for assembly in 1993–1994.

In the subway portions downtown, doors are electronically operated by driver. At street-level stops, press down on metal handrails to open doors. Be *very* careful of oncoming traffic. You may hear bells ringing at times, too. This is a warning signal given when passenger steps in each car are raised as the train reaches the subway-level platforms.

In downtown stations, money is placed into turnstiles, or pass or transfer is shown to station agent before descending to track level. The BART/Muni map gives complete route information for each train, and there are large maps in each station and on some cars.

Tip to Travelers: If outbound Market Street trains are too busy to board, backtrack to Embarcadero Station on the train you'll be riding. At this station trains simply reverse direction—you'll find yourself "at the head of the class."

Muni Buses and Trolleys

The Muni bus fleet is made up of both gas-powered and electric-overhead trolley buses. Over 525 buses are in operation and 36 articulated trolleys will join the fleet in 1992 and 1993.

Buses operate 6 a.m. - 1 a.m. daily, with some all-night "owl" service. Consult your BART/Muni map for late-night owl routes in service.

Fare for adults is $1.00, payable in exact change only. Muni operators do not carry change, although many buses are being equipped with machines that can handle paper money. Other boarding methods include passes and transfers. Transfers are given when boarding the bus. (If you aren't offered one, ask.) When boarding a bus with a pass or transfer, offer it face up to the driver.

Transfers are good twice, in any direction, within the 1–2 hour time limit noted at the transfer tear-off. Driver will tear off first-use portion of transfer, or if that's already used up, will take the remaining transfer from you. If transfer is expired, you will have to pay again. When you reach your stop, tell driver or operate the stop requesting cords or press-bars. When you exit a bus, look both directions before stepping down.

Take the F Line...
PCC Streetcars Return

Market Street will be well-served by a new trolley car line, the F Line. The fleet of restored PCC cars will replace the #8 Market Street electric bus route. The track-guided, overhead wire-powered PCC line will be up and running by 1994; the entire planned system will be in place by 1996, including Fisherman's Wharf and Fremont Street termini. The first leg will travel between The Castro and The Ferry Building.

Muni purchased 20 refurbished PCC's from the City of Philadelphia, which they'll combine with SF's 45 PCC's that are being refitted for service. At least 12 PCC's will operate at once on Market Street.

PCC is an abbreviation for Electric Railway Presidents' Conference Committee. The first PCC was built in 1936 as an attempt by transit companies to reverse the decline in public transportation ridership. To sum it up, Muni is jumping "back to the future" in the reestablishment of the reliable, dependable and very popular PCC transit vehicles in The City.

According to Chief Equipment Engineer, Bob Highfill, "There is an overwhelming emotional sentiment about these street cars in the transit industry. Other cities are calling us, wanting to do the same thing." Bravo Muni!

"The St. Louis Car" PCC

Airport Transportation

China Clipper over
the Golden Gate, 1937

Although there is no BART service to
SFO, San Francisco's colossal international airport, there are many affordable and convenient alternatives. Most
travelers prefer the door-to-door airport shuttles, which generally require
at least three hours notice for scheduling your home pick-up. Here are many:

Airport Connection
Airport service in San Francisco, East
Bay and Peninsula, under $20.
Call 1-800-877-0901 for information.

Easy-Way Out
Door-to-door airport service to Oakland
Airport from SF, under $20.
Call (510) 887-6226.

Lorrie's Airport Shuttle
Door-to-door airport service to and from
SFO daily, about $20.
Call 334-9000 for pick-ups.

Marin Airporter
North Bay service to and from SFO.
Call 461-4222 for information.

SF Airporter
Service between SFO and downtown
hotels, 5 a.m. to midnight, under $10.
Pick-up every 20 minutes, departing
from Hyatt Regency Hotel at 5 Embarcadero, California and Market Streets
(least expensive practical way to SFO).

Super Shuttle
Door-to-door airport service 24 hours
daily, about $15. To travel to SFO call
558-8500. From SFO call 871-7800.

Yellow Airport Service
Door-to-door 24-hour service to and
from SF and Oakland airports. Call
282-RIDE for pick-ups.

*For your reference, a taxi from down-
town SF to SFO will cost just under $25
with tip. Travel time to SFO from The
City is about 20–45 minutes, depending on traffic. Ride-sharing lowers fares.
(See list of Taxi Cabs on Page 203.)
Prices listed above are approximate.
Call for exact charges. Tips are generally 15–20% of fare.

Trains, Regional Buses & Bicycles

Amtrak offers: *The Coast Starlight*, traveling between San Diego and Seattle; *The California Zephyr*, traveling between Oakland and Chicago via Reno, Salt Lake City and Denver; *The Capitol* to Sacramento and other routes throughout California and beyond.

For information on routes and fares call **1-800-USA-RAIL**. Amtrak service has improved greatly in recent months following sweeping internal changes. Amtrak offers a full range of passes and "See America" multi-week fares. SF passengers meet at Transbay Terminal at 1st & Mission and are whisked to the Amtrak Depot in Oakland by special buses (Amtrak trains do not enter San Francisco).

CalTrain offers train service down the peninsula to San Jose and points enroute. Call 1-800-558-8661 for schedule and fare info.

Greyhound/Trailways Bus Lines are boarded at Transbay Terminal, 1st & Mission. Greyhound/Trailways offers complete service to Nevada destinations including Reno, Sparks and Lake Tahoe. Call 558-6789 for Greyhound routes and fares.

San Mateo County Transit (SamTrans) buses travel within San Mateo and Palo Alto, with service in South San Francisco. They offer a broad-based package of commuter services, transfer services and special Candlestick Park, San Francisco Airport and Bay Meadows Racetrack routes. A wide selection of passes is available for the frequent traveler on SamTrans lines throughout the greater peninsula area. Call SamTrans at 761-7000 in San Francisco.

Golden Gate Transit buses and ferries travel between Marin County and San Francisco. Call GGT, 332-6600, for boarding locations, fares and schedules (see also *The Bay Ferries*, next page).

AC Transit is the East Bay's bus service, with transbay service to SF's Transbay Terminal at 1st & Mission. AC Transit offers the same service package as Muni, including passes and transfers. Call AC Transit at 839-2882 to receive maps and schedules by mail.

The Bay Ferries

Ferry-to-Bus Transfers

Passengers can transfer to bus service from all ferries, with transfers often included in ticket price. Some ferries, such as the ever-popular Alcatraz service, require advance reservation. Ask the agent. There is a full menu of ferry commuter passes available, too. The ferries have become more popular for commuting. Many switched to them after the Quake of '89 stopped both BART and Bay Bridge service; once the emergency was over, they never went back to their old ways. Pets can usually make the trip, call. Dress warmly for Bay crossings.

CALTRANS Bike Shuttle/ Transbay Service

SF: Transbay Terminal
Treasure Island: Bay Bridge Bus Stops
Oakland: MacArthur BART Station

Weekday Mornings: Leave Oakland 6:20, 7:00, 7:45, 8:30. Leave SF 6:40, 7:25, 8:10.

Weekday Evenings: Leave Oakland 3:50, 4:40, 5:30, 6:15. Leave SF 4:15, 5:05, 5:55.

Fare, bike and rider one-way, $1.00. Call 923-4444 or 464-0876 for more information.

Golden Gate Transit operates daily ferry service from SF's Ferry Building to Larkspur Landing and Sausalito in Marin County. Passenger fare ranges from $2.20–$3.50 one-way, with fares discounted for kids, seniors and disabled persons. Ships leave both sides every hour or so; call 332-6600 for schedule. Coats and sweaters are a must for all Bay crossings.

The Red & White Fleet operates daily passenger service to Alameda, Oakland (Jack London Waterfront), Tiburon, Vallejo and Sausalito. There are Red & White ferries traveling to Alcatraz Island and Angel Island; a Bay cruise is also available. Adult fares range from $3.50 to $14.00 for the scenic cruise; kids and seniors receive substantial discounts. Call The Red & White Fleet at 1-800-445-8880 or 546-BOAT from SF. Ships depart SF from The Ferry Building at the foot of Market Street and from Pier 41 at Fisherman's Wharf. Bicycles can be accommodated on all ferries. Call for complete details.

The Blue & Gold Fleet offers Bay scenic cruises departing from Pier 39. These 75-minute-long cruises take in the waterfront of San Francisco and both of SF's famous bridges. Call 781-8788 for details.

Automobiles

Car owners in San Francisco have a few special things to bear in mind. There's even a book about SF's most affordable, City-owned garages downtown. Parking in The City is a challenge!

Out-of-state licenses are good in California for one year. Call the Department of Motor Vehicles at 557-1191 for driver's license information. (The DMV is located at the east end of the panhandle between Oak and Fell.) Arrive early for fastest service. Call for hours; appointment suggested.

A warning to City newcomers: Upon application for your California license, the DMV will confiscate your out-of-state license and give you a non-photo ID for driving. You will not receive your oh-so-snazzy photo license for 2–3 months. This can cause problems cashing checks and opening bank accounts. Plan around this delay...

Curbing your wheels: When parked on steep grades, turn your car's wheels into curb to prevent runaways. Apply hand brake. This is the law, not just a good idea, particularly on Nob Hill. Tickets are handed out for this.

Neighborhood parking permits, which allow neighborhood residents to park all day in their neighborhood's two-hour parking zones without being ticketed, are available from The City. Call 554-4466 for information. *For some helpful recorded City parking information call 558-6455.*

The Berkeley **Trip Commute Store** offers transit passes, carpool match-ups, maps, schedules and more. The store is located at 2033 Center Street, below Shattuck in Berkeley, and is open weekdays 8:30 a.m. - 5:30 p.m. Call (510) 644-POOL.

Rides for Bay Area Commuters, at 60 Spear Street, offers a free ride-matching service for Bay Area employers. Call 861-7665 for pool van and car information. They also buy and sell $500 cars to regular commuter pools.

Curbs are painted to denote parking laws:

Red: No stopping or parking, ever.
Yellow: Half-hour loading zones, vehicles with permits only. Fair game after 6 p.m.
Yellow & Black: Same as above, but limited to trucks.
Blue: Disabled parking only, 24 hours daily.
Green: Ten-minute limit, Mon.-Sat. 8 a.m. – 6 p.m.
White: Five-minute limit while adjoining business is open. Fair game at other times.

California law allows left turns on red from a one-way into another one-way, if coast is clear and turn is begun from far left lane only. This is a law many Easterners might not be aware of.

The Boot: The San Francisco Parking and Traffic Commission has purchased over 150 "Denver Boots" and employs nine full-time workers to use them. **Car owners who leave their car parked on the street with 5 (five) or more unpaid parking tickets risk having their car "booted,"** which renders the car immovable, and for all intents and purposes is as ugly as being towed. You will have to go to 850 Bryant Street (open weekdays 8:30 a.m. - 4:30 p.m.) to pay your outstanding parking tickets. A $50 "booting fee" will be tacked on. *Brand new law—five tickets—keep tickets paid up! Also, bus stops cost $100 now...*

Getting Towed

No one lives in SF very long without having their car towed. To retrieve it, you must clear any parking fines at the Police Station at 850 Bryant Street between the hours of 8 a.m. and 4:30 p.m. The next stop is City Tow (1475 Mission, 621-8605) which, hopefully, has your car. Try to wait patiently, then pay the more than $100 towing fee and any additional storage fees to get your car back.

All this will take half a day or so. Make no other plans, or you may be disappointed. The only way to avoid this little bit of hell is to keep your tickets paid up, never park illegally or block a driveway and pay utmost attention to Tow-Away Zones, indicated by signs. Many streets allow parking except at rush hours; at these times tow trucks descend upon hapless cars like swarming locusts!

A skilled tow truck driver can "hook" your car in less than two minutes. Once the front wheels leave the ground, there's no argument. Beware! Also, the SF Police Department does spot checks for parking scofflaws on randomly chosen streets, using handheld computers. Keep tickets paid up! **Call 553-1235 for towed-car info.**

Let's Park in San Francisco!

by Kenneth Fried

Ah, San Francisco! City of ethnic diversity and a unique variety of lifestyles and opinions. But all its citizens agree on one thing: the parking stinks!

Why so bad? Unlike, say, Los Angeles, San Francisco was built up before the private car became the popular way to get around. And as the population grew, the number of cars grew with it, but crowded City streets didn't. Rental cars and cars from sprouting suburbs arrived. And then the tourists came...

That's pretty much it, today. They've built garages, shortened parking spaces, hired more control officers, bought more Denver Boots and ticketed and towed more scofflaws. But as long as regional transit remains inadequate, gas is cheap and City residents decline to allow parking garages to be built on their block, parking remains difficult.

What to do? Sell the car. Walk. Bike. Move to Idaho...Stop! Pick up the book that lays out all the parking options, written by a local who felt he'd been fleeced once too often by an overpriced parking garage.

Let's Park in San Francisco maps out on-street parking regulations and parking garages, lists their prices and hours and includes parking maps of areas where free parking is usually but a dream: North Beach, Chinatown, the Marina and the Haight. The book also includes the Financial District, Union Square and other difficult-to-park neighborhoods. It even includes SFO.

Let's Park in San Francisco introduces comparison shopping to the world of parking. A single use covers the cost of the book—$5.95, half the price of a parking ticket. Want to avoid having the judge throw the book at you? Toss this book into your glove compartment. It fits.

Kenneth Fried's book, Let's Park in San Francisco, *is published by Heyday Books in Berkeley. Call (510) 536-3564.*

Taxi Cabs

American Cab Co.	775-3377
Arrow Cab Co.	564-6911
Blue Bird Cab Co.	664-5800
Central Cab Co.	474-2919
City Cabs	468-7200
Daly City Cabs	992-8865
De Soto Cab Co.	673-1414
Diamond Cabs	826-9588
Golden Cab Co.	864-5194
King Cabs	567-9839
Lucky Cab Co.	752-0898
Luxor Cabs	282-4141
National Cab Co.	648-4444
Pacific Cab Co.	986-7220
State Cab Co.	392-1785
Sunshine Cab	776-7755
Universal Cab Company	334-1384
Veterans' Taxicab Co.	552-1300
Yellow Cab Company	626-2345

This is a fairly complete list. Some companies are large, some small. Everyone has their favorites.

Quick Directory

These are frequently dialed transit numbers. More information is contained elsewhere in this section.

AAA Membership Info.	565-2012
AAA Car Towing	863-3432
AC Transit	(510) 839-2882
TTY#	(510) 465-5295
Amtrak	1-800-872-7245
Bay Bridge Info.	464-1148
BART	788-BART
TTY#	839-2218
Disabled	464-7133
Blue & Gold Fleet	781-7877
California Road Conditions	557-3755
CalTrain	557-8661 or 495-4546
Golden Gate Bridge	921-5858
Golden Gate Transit	332-6600
(Buses & Ferries)	
Greyhound/Trailways	558-6789
Muni General Info.	673-MUNI
TTY#	558-2336
Lost & Found (M-F 12-5)	923-6168
Senior ID (M-F 8-5)	626-1033
Disabled 923-6142 or 923-6070	
Complaints (M-F 8-5)	923-6164
Oakland Airport	(510) 577-4015
Passport Information	974-7972
SamTrans	761-7000
Santa Clara Co. Tr.	(408) 965-3100
TTY#	(408) 299-4848
SF Airport	761-0800

Consult airlines directly for passenger flight information. See your telephone directory under "Airlines." There are over 100 carriers serving SFO.

THE GRAVEN IMAGE GRAPHICS

THE GRAVEN IMAGE GRAPHICS is proud of its role in bringing you this year's ALMANAC. But THE ALMANAC is just one of the many projects we've worked on. Graven Image artist Elizabeth is also the co-creator of **A Book Lover's Guide To The Mission,** *the map of Mission District bookstores featured in* **Books, Paper & Ink.**

The Graven Image Graphics provides full-service editing, illustration, design and desktop publishing. We have a large library of typefaces to fit your every design need. We can work with clients large and small to assure quality at an affordable price. From résumés to advertisements to full-length books, we are ready to serve you. Call us!

Elizabeth Newman is a graphic artist with 15 years of experience. She has illustration, design and pre-production experience on projects big and small. Elizabeth created original illustrations, designed advertisements and did desktop publishing for this year's ALMANAC.

Michael Koenig has five years of editing experience, with a journalism background. He wrote and edited a company newsletter and created proposals, charts and graphics on computer. Michael did copyediting and desktop publishing for this year's ALMANAC.

---

648 Beacon Street #6 ▼ *Oakland, CA 94610* ▼ *(510) 452-4990*

THE GRAVEN IMAGE GRAPHICS

▼ **Illustration**

▼ **Design**

▼ **Typesetting**

▼ **Production**

▼ **Editing & Proofreading**

Elizabeth Newman
Michael Koenig
648 Beacon St. #6
Oakland,
CA 94610
(510) 452-4990

The Signs of the Zodiac

 1. Aries the ram (head) —March 21st-April 19th

 2. Taurus the bull (neck) —April 20th-May 20th

 3. Gemini the twins (arms)—May 21st-June 20th

 4. Cancer the crab (breast)—June 21st-July 22nd

 5. Leo the lion (heart) —July 23rd-August 22nd

 6. Virgo the virgin (belly) — August 23rd-September 22nd

 7. Libra the balance (reins) — September 23rd-October 22nd

 8. Scorpio the scorpion (secrets) — October 23rd-November 21st

 9. Sagittarius the archer (thighs) — November 22nd-December 21st

 10. Capricornus the goat (knees) —December 22nd-January 19th

 11. Aquarius the water-bearer (legs) — January 20th-February 18th

 12. Pisces the fish (feet) —February 19th-March 20th

We would like to thank all the fine artists who created the artwork in this ALMANAC. Original illustrations are by The Graven Image's talented artist Elizabeth Newman. Many WPA and *San Franciscan* magazine (1921-1929) drawings, sketches and doodles are included. (This handy horoscope wheel was created by a WPA artist in 1940 for a wartime guidebook of San Francisco.) We have also used a selection of Dover Books' fine clips. To all the talented artists, known and unknown, we extend our gratitude and thanks...

ALMANAC INDEX

THE SAN FRANCISCO ALMANAC Index

THE SAN FRANCISCO ALMANAC **Index**

†Sponsors are indicated in italic type. ††Bold type indicates feature section.

(back page)

**San Francisco's
Native Wisdom!**

Would you like to include your fine shop, business, service or organization in our very next planned ALMANAC edition? Please call the Editor, Walter Biller, at (415) 751-0657 or call (800) 352-5268. We are always pleased to hear from our community.

**ALMANAC purchase includes two issues of our biannual newsletter, *The Almanac News.* The Spring/Summer issue is mailed in June/July and a Fall/Winter issue is mailed before Christmas. *The Almanac News* will also be available in shops, bookstores and other locations in San Francisco.

***Don't forget!* Send in your free *Almanac News* back-page mailer so we can include you on our reader mailing list...

✍ Notes

Mail in Your *Free* *ALMANAC NEWS* Subscription Order Today!

Mail this coupon to:

- - - - - - - - - - - - - - - - - -

THE SAN FRANCISCO ALMANAC NEWS
1657 Waller Street #A
San Francisco, California 94117

▼   ▼

You'll receive (at least) two (2) biannual issues of our FREE reader newsletter, *THE ALMANAC NEWS,* included with your ALMANAC purchase.

Name _____

Mailing Address _____

_____

_____

Please note that we have enclosed
Friends of the SF Public Library
membership envelopes in this issue.
This is to help Friends to continue to
find new members in this critical era
for our public libraries.

If your provided Friends envelope
didn't make it, call Friends of the
Library at 557-4257 to receive one.

*Almanac News mailers, to avoid any
confusion, should be sent to The
Almanac in your envelope. Thanks.*